INSIGHT-LED SELLING

INSIGHT-LED SELLING

ADOPT AN EXECUTIVE MINDSET,

BUILD CREDIBILITY,

COMMUNICATE WITH IMPACT

DR. STEPHEN G. TIMME
and MELODY ASTLEY

LIONCREST
PUBLISHING

INSIGHT-LED SELLING

Adopt an Executive Mindset, Build Credibility, Communicate with Impact

ISBN	978-1-5445-2220-3	*Hardcover*
	978-1-5445-2219-7	*Paperback*
	978-1-5445-2218-0	*Ebook*
	978-1-5445-2221-0	*Audiobook*

From Stephen, to my wife, Lisa, my son Will, and my parents, Mary Ellen and Bill Timme.

And from Melody, to my mother, Marcia Ross, and my sister, Autumn Maloy.

CONTENTS

INTRODUCTION

"Bring me something fresh from the outside—something I don't know. Show me that you've not only identified one of my problems, but you have a fresh solution that you've implemented somewhere else that will work for me too."

—**STEVE CLANCEY,** CIO, Georgia Pacific

The sales profession is not for the faint of heart. But you know that. Here's something you may not know:

According to Forbes, *in 2017 a whopping 57 percent of sellers missed their quota.*[1]

We wanted to know why. Why do smart, well-trained people who work hard continue to come up short on their sales goals? Like all good salespeople, we started by looking at the problem from the customer's point of view:

---

1   Shep Hyken, "57% of Sales Reps Missed Their Quotas Last Year," Forbes.com, September 2, 2018, https://www.forbes.com/sites/shephyken/2018/09/02/77-of-sales-reps-missed-their-quotas-last-year/.

Seventy-seven percent of buyers say that sellers do not understand their business.[2]

This, we believe, is the key, and it's what this whole book is about: Helping sellers to see their products and services from the buyer's point of view. Teaching them how to walk in the customer's shoes and speak their language. Ultimately, showing sellers how to determine the impact their solution has on their customers' business and how to communicate that information in a way the customer hears and understands.

Vendors making a significant impact on a buyer's business get a 31 percent higher share of wallet than other vendors.[3]

A 31 percent higher share of wallet could go a long way toward closing that gap for the 57 percent of salespeople who miss their quota. For the other 43 percent, it could blow their quota out of the water. This isn't a sales trick. It's not a sales process. It's how to build credibility and confidence, and how to be more impactful early on. And despite what you might believe, it's 100 percent possible.

WHAT'S GOING ON
WITH SALES TEAMS?

When's the last time you told your Sales leadership, "You know, I really think you need to raise my quota—it's just too darn low"?

---

2   Doug Winter, "How Well Do Your Salespeople Understand Your Buyers?" Bizjournals.com, February 13, 2015, https://www.bizjournals.com/bizjournals/how-to/marketing/2015/02/how-well-do-your-salespeople-understand-buyers.html.

3   "Analytics and Advice for B2B Leaders," Gallup.com, 2017, https://www.gallup.com/analytics/267998/advice-for-b2b-leaders.aspx.

Probably never. Every salesperson thinks their quota is too high. That thought gets in your head, and the more you believe it, the harder it is for you to sell. And when you consistently struggle to make your number and don't see a clear path for making it, you tend to get discouraged. Some salespeople get so frustrated that they believe the only solution is moving to another company. But then, you have to learn a whole new line of products, and it probably isn't any better—or easier to sell—than the line of products at your last company.

It's hard on you and it's hard on your customers. You would like to build a better relationship with them over time and get to know their business. They'd like to work with a salesperson who sticks around long enough to learn their business and help them reach their operational goals, financial goals, and expected business outcomes.

WHAT'S GOING ON WITH EXECUTIVES?

All this leads to slower sales, missed quotas, and lost revenue. Sales leaders would love to explain all this to the CFO, the CEO, and everyone else who's looking at them to deliver that big number, but ultimately, Sales leadership is still accountable, and it's their problem.

Executives have shareholders or investors to satisfy, salaries to pay, and projects to fund. They have a number hanging over their heads, too, and Sales leaders and sellers are likely the biggest part of that number.

Publicly traded companies in particular have aggregated quotas close to their budgets. They're not building in a

50 percent fudge factor. When your company plans against a certain budget but doesn't generate enough sales, there are tradeoffs like underfunded or canceled projects—even layoffs. And the margin between hitting and not hitting the number is slim.

When the 2020 coronavirus pandemic hit, a lot of companies stopped giving earnings-per-share (EPS) guidance due to the uncertainty. If you look at what they were putting out there before that time, you'd see the spread might be just 10 cents. They'd announce they were planning to make between $3.00 and $3.10, and some spreads were even tighter. If they were off by a penny, investors would punish them for a long time, which is why a lot of companies did crazy things such as cut back on research and development (R&D), avoid nonessential travel, and even lay off their salesforces—*the revenue-generating engines.* There's a lot of pressure on executives to make shareholders happy.

When it comes to hitting sales quotas, executives aren't going to budge. The answer, then, has to come from Sales and what they can do differently to better connect with their customers and give them what they want.

Sales and Sales leadership are accountable, but it's not an easy problem to solve. Sales leaders want their people to succeed. They want their sellers to feel enriched and find meaning in their work. But when you aren't making quota, you feel your angst and your management's angst too. Being part of a sales team that isn't doing well is stressful, and the only solution is to figure out how to sell better. Yet, you've been in training for years, even decades. It didn't seem to be this hard in the past, so what's changed? Why isn't what you always did in the past working anymore?

THE SOLUTION

"The salesperson should be more interested in learning about my business, instead of telling me about theirs. Unless they care about what matters to me right now and are forward-thinking enough to find out what's going to be important to me in the future, I am not going to care about what they can do and will care even less about the details of their solution.

> "What's sad is how many sellers don't do it right. Even senior-level sellers have forgotten how to be 'external'—customer focused. Most are just dumping data, and no one wants to be data dumped."
>
> **—DEAN Z. MYERS,** President, DZM Consulting and former VP Global Supply Chain, Operations and Business Development, The Coca-Cola Company. DeanZMyersConsulting.com

The good news is, there is a solution, and it's not as complicated or difficult as you might think. The key is getting to know your customer better—their business, their industry, and the various stakeholders involved in the buying decision process. It's making the effort to learn how they measure success. If you're going to ask them to spend money with you, you need to be able to show how your solution can help them achieve their goals, implement their strategies, and ultimately deliver their desired business outcomes.

This is what Insight-Led Selling is all about. It empowers you to address the goals that are most critical to executives with business benefits such as enhanced customer experience and financial benefits such as improved revenue. These add up to what executives are really looking for, which is a best-case business outcome.

Once you have these insights, you can use that skill forever. It will not become obsolete. It's always relevant, in every industry, across the board. We are here to give you a repeatable, scalable framework, and once you understand the fundamentals, you can implement it with every customer, in any industry. Once you start having conversations based on this framework, you will see a positive revenue impact.

The buyer pie is only so big in a given year. Someone's getting the share, and it might as well be you. Following this framework will help you transform buyer perceptions. Customers will see that you're different—that you *do* understand them. In turn, you'll net a higher percentage of wallet share and eliminate the competition. Because the majority of your competition is getting it all wrong. Put yourself in the high-performing minority, win the mindshare of the customer, and you'll win the wallet share. Once you have buyer allegiance, they'll want to keep talking to you, not take a cold call from the seller who shows no insight into their business and its needs.

By the end of this book, you'll know how to have more business-focused conversations with buyers by having greater customer insights. You'll be able to do your homework regarding their goals and strategies and how they're performing financially, and you'll understand their industry headwinds and tailwinds and how your solutions deliver business outcomes, allowing you to tailor your conversations more effectively. You can visit InsightLedSelling.com for resources that will help you more quickly apply what you learn in this book. Use the code INSIGHTSELLER to access the site.

To build a positive relationship and become the go-to seller, you need specific, concrete insights around the buyer's goals and strategies. For instance, you might find out they are trying to reduce operating expense to invest more in the business and fuel top-line growth. Then the question becomes, what do you do? Our framework will help you map your solutions to a customer's goals and strategies. Similarly, you'll learn to identify your customer's top three Areas of Financial Performance. We'll help you come up with a clear explanation of how your solutions impact one or more of those financial areas. Part of looking at financial performance is figuring out exactly whom you're selling to and what their metrics are. Then you'll craft a story about how you can help them get there.

Industry headwinds and tailwinds are a way of thinking about challenges and opportunities. COVID-19 is an obvious example of a headwind for a traditional retail space but maybe a tailwind for a company like Amazon. A headwind for consumer products might be a retailer trend toward private label. A tailwind could be using technology to enhance buyer experience. Your role might be to explain how you could help with that transition.

All your research and thinking about the buyer's perspective leads to a tailored message to each individual buyer that demonstrates the business and financial benefits of your solution in a clear, compelling way. We call this stage the How and How Much. We provide a way for you to have this conversation and ultimately explain how your solutions deliver business outcomes and how much your solutions will add to the top line—your client's sales—and the bottom line, their profits.

To supplement what we know, we also interviewed executive buyers for their perspectives. Many of them, such as Steve Clancey, Dean Z. Myers, and Candy Conway, graciously allowed us to quote them in the pages of this book.

> *"To be a better seller, have a strong story. Tell me how this is all going to work so I 'get it' right away. Be prepared for me not to like your initial proposal too. If it doesn't work for me and I tell you why, be ready to adjust and propose something different.*
>
> *"Most of all, follow up. I can't say that enough. Few sellers follow up as often or as long as executive buyers need them to. We're busy, and we need to be reminded of what a seller talked to us about the last time, and we need to be updated on what's next. I appreciate a call that starts off with, 'Hey, Candy, remember the last time we talked about this. Now I need to ask you about this.' A good seller can do this without being obnoxious about it.*
>
> *"So, have a strong story going in, be ready to adjust and adapt, and follow up. Sounds like Sales 101, right? Yet most sellers fail on one, two, or all three steps."*
>
> **—CANDY CONWAY,**
> former VP Global Operations, AT&T

WHERE WE CAME FROM

As a professor of finance at Emory University and Georgia State University and an instructor at the Georgia Institute of Technology, Stephen, a PhD in Finance, had the opportunity to work with many different companies. His conversations usually began with a finance group intent on improving operations. Stephen would help folks in different lines of business (or business units) such as operations, sales, and marketing understand how they impacted their business on a day-to-day basis and the business and financial benefits of new projects. While teaching an open enrollment workshop at Georgia Tech, a software company seller approached him about applying his ideas in a sales environment.

Here was their reasoning: Sellers have the challenge of explaining how their solutions improve performance and by how much just like people in different lines of business have to do internally. If that's how companies manage performance, so too should a seller think that way when talking about the benefits of their solutions. Stephen started getting engagements in the early '90s, and by the early 2000s, he began focusing on sales organizations. Having worked for major *Fortune* 500s, Stephen brings clear, insider insights around how companies make decisions. Here, he takes that real-world experience to the other side of the table to help sellers be much more relevant.

Melody, a career-long seller and sales leader, spent twelve years at IBM and used this framework as a client executive, including having a large matrix team supporting a financial services customer with an aggregate quota of more than $150 million. She knows firsthand that the framework in this book works because she used it and made her numbers.

Together, we have a clear sense of what both sides of the table need and how to get sellers to connect with buyers by offering real value—specifically, to improve the financial performance of their company. We know how to quickly get customers' attention and tell them something they don't already know, deliver business outcomes, show them how we can make their life easier, and often, help them think about an issue in a way they haven't before.

We know from experience there's real frustration on the buyer side, caused by both external vendors trying to sell and internal marketers asking for more money. That frustration comes out in all kinds of interesting behavior, from customers saying, "Tell me something I don't know in three minutes or this meeting is over," to simply starting to laugh, signaling the seller's time is up. Sales can be a brutal business if you don't approach it in the right way.

You think about the buyer a hundred times more than they think about you; they're not waking up wondering, *what can I do to help my vendors?* You have a small window to forge the right relationship. Doing so takes a framework—you can't just leave it to chance and expect to succeed. There's a lot of competition out there and only so many hours in a week. Executives don't want to take extra meetings. In order to get your time with them, you have to demonstrate you're bringing value that's worth cutting some other meeting out of the schedule. No one is going to voluntarily cede you that time slot, so you have to earn it. Succeeding means gaining mindshare and impacting your customer's performance. You have to be relevant, or buyers won't have time for you.

LET'S GET STARTED

This book outlines a framework, not a methodology. It's agnostic as far as any values-based sales process, and it fits with what you're currently doing. If you're already using a methodology, great. Our framework will not override or displace it.

We understand you already have a sales method in place that probably breaks into opportunity, identification, and pursuit planning or something similar. It might be off-the-shelf or custom-made for your organization. Our framework builds upon what you've already invested in. We help enhance every step of the sales process, from discovery all the way to post-sale and value realization.

This book isn't an MBA crash course, and you don't need to be a financial expert—or even have an advanced degree—to understand it. We understand sellers, which metrics are relevant, and which insights matter to executives. We do the heavy lifting so you don't have to worry about all the calculations. We'll touch on them a little bit, but the whole point is to simplify what might otherwise be an intimidating topic. We want to make you comfortable so you can be more effective. We want you to walk away with a blueprint that you can repeat and scale so you can start seeing results right away. This information is essential to sales, and it's a crying shame they don't typically teach it in business school. It would save a lot of executives, sales leaders, and salespeople a lot of grief.

Let's start at the top, with the executives. Not yours—your customers'. Because if you can decode what the top decision makers care about, you will be better at showing the business outcomes benefits of your solutions.

EXECUTIVE INSIGHTS

"I expect sellers to understand our products, our brand, and our business. They should listen to the earnings call, review the investor presentation, learn our goals, and know what our CEO cares about. Sellers who do that really stand out, and even if their solution isn't a good fit for my project, I'll refer them to other people in my company and even people in other companies."

—JO ANN HEROLD, Chief Marketing Officer,
The Honey Baked Ham Company

A sales VP at one of the largest global technology companies once told the story of meeting Lee Iacocca, the Chrysler CEO credited with saving the automobile company in the 1980s. The VP told Iacocca about all the solutions his company offered, but he seemed unimpressed. Then the VP's wife spoke up to tell Iacocca how they'd just purchased a Chrysler minivan, which she loved, and that she had a few ideas for making it even better. In the end, Iacocca gave the woman his card and told her to call him if she had any other suggestions. *He completely ignored her husband, the VP!*

To sell to executives, you must think like an executive. You need to tailor the message of the business and financial benefits of your solutions in a way that addresses their needs, interests, and issues—not yours—and gains their trust.

Imagine you're an executive looking at a mountainous pile of work that needs your attention. The last thing you want to do is have a pointless meeting with a vendor who just wants to sell you something and doesn't understand your main problems and sources of stress or how to fix them. That's essentially how Iacocca felt about the VP's generic pitch. Now imagine a seller approaches you and says, "I know the top three items on your to-do list, why they're so hard, and how to help you cross them off with much less stress." Suddenly, you'd have plenty of time for that meeting, right? The VP's wife, with targeted suggestions based on user experience, represented much more value to Chrysler, even though she wasn't there to pitch anything.

Having executive insights affords these advantages:

- Puts you in the buyer's mindset so you can understand what they value

- Allows you to have a more impactful business-focused conversation with decision makers

- Leads to additional opportunities by taking a more holistic view of the customer

SALES LANGUAGE AT THE EXECUTIVE LEVEL

The Iacocca story clearly illustrates that there's a right way and a wrong way to speak to executives, and you absolutely must do your homework. You have to talk to them about what matters to them, not you nor your company. They care about their business, their products, and their customers. Mostly, they care about achieving business outcomes, which include both operational improvements and gains in financial performance. And it's not enough to just "know the numbers." You also have to translate those numbers into information that gets an executive's attention and actually *matters* to them: their goals, strategies, initiatives, and ultimately, expected business outcomes. Finally, you have to lead with what's important to the executive buyer before you start rolling out any numbers at all.

Although the goals of executive stakeholders may align with the company's goals (such as improving profitability), how each stakeholder gets there differs with initiatives often unique to the department. You need to know how they think, what their goals and key metrics are, why business and financial value matters to them, and how to talk to them.

You can't just assume you're talking to the right person either because roles and budgets have changed and are still changing. For example, titles such as Chief Digital Officer and Chief Customer Care Officer didn't exist not so many years ago. In the tech space, as much as 50 percent of IT spend historically owned by the CIO's office is now allocated to other departments. Lines of business such as marketing, sales, operations, and supply chain management make technology purchases to increase revenue, improve profitability, and manage assets. That proportion represents a huge shift, and you need to think like your executive buyers and tailor your approach and language to the mindset of each individual.

Missed Opportunity

Surveys by our company, FinListics, and one of our partners that develops account visualization software, Revegy, shown in Figure 1-1, "How Well Does Your Sales Force Know Their Customers?" turned up these disappointing facts:

- Only 19 percent of Sales managers believe their sellers are trusted advisors.

- Nearly a third, 31 percent, think their sellers still focus on features and functions.

- A full 50 percent of the same managers said their people know the customer's goals but struggle to align their solutions to those goals.

Insights into not only the goals of executive buyers within a single line of business but also those of other business units and tailoring your message accordingly represents a huge opportunity. Making the most of this environment of disbursed budgets requires learning to interact with executives who probably don't speak the language you're accustomed to using.

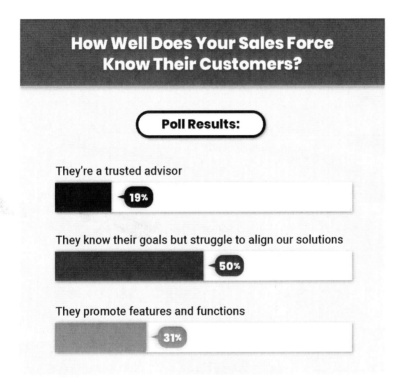

Figure 1-1. How Well Does Your Sales Force Know Their Customers? Our poll provided some disappointing results about Sales' customer insights.

WHAT EXECUTIVES REALLY WANT FROM YOU

"First, I expect a sales professional to know my industry. Who else is selling into my industry? What differentiates this seller from their competition and how can they offer me a better value?

"Second, know my business and how the product is made. If they're new, they should avail themselves of an education. I do not want to hear how great their company is or all about their product, especially if they know nothing about mine.

"Third, I want the seller to be my advocate. Sales reps know this because I tell them, 'I have to be transparent with you and I have to trust you. I'm expecting you to be almost a pain in the side inside your company on my behalf.' If I hear complaints from their leadership about how strongly the seller is supporting me, then I know they're doing their job."

—BILL CORTNER, President, Cortner Consulting, LLC, and
former Director, Procter & Gamble Prchases
and VP, J.M. Smucker Company

Our research for this book included many interviews with executive buyers to provide perspectives from the other side of the desk or virtual sales call. What we learned confirmed what we believed from our own experiences—that executive buyers want three main things from you, the seller:

1. First, they want to learn something from you that they don't already know.

2. They also want you to demonstrate how your solutions can help them achieve their desired business outcomes. This is typically accomplished by improving operational performance, perhaps through greater efficiency, agility, and resiliency, which leads to improved financial performance.

3. Finally, they want you to make their life easier. Executives are constantly fielding input internally. Sometimes they need your expert advice to sort through the noise and help them choose the best move.

Giving an executive buyer what they want benefits the seller as much as the buyer. By knowing their business and satisfying these three requirements, you'll build credibility. You'll also begin to see the buyer's problem or goal—and their strategies and initiatives for solving that problem or reaching that goal—from *their* point of view. The clearer you are on their perspective, the easier it will be for you to empathize with them and actually care about helping them. Instead of just trying to sell them something, you'll become invested in their success. Being an advocate for your buyer can lead to a deal for you and a better business outcome for them. Let's talk about how you get there.

Tell Them Something They Don't Know

"As anyone leading a company or division might attest, whether you're in finance or otherwise, our full-time jobs are packed with both planned and unplanned responsibilities. At times, it can be a stressful game of triage. Even though I like to keep an open mind, it's difficult and unappealing to prioritize a sales call from even the nicest person, so I may only give it a sliver of my time and headspace.

"If I'm going to allocate my time to a buying decision, I can't afford for it to become a big project. I need the seller to spoon-feed me the critical items and answer

my questions without me having to ask them, 'What will this do for me (problem-solution clarity), and what are its limitations? What's the all-in price for the offering?' Once that all settles into my consciousness, I can consider it, but I need that total transparency right away. I just don't have time for lengthy back-and-forth emails, calls, and homework."

—NATHAN DANE, CFO, Intent Solutions

Imagine your customer, a retailer, is expanding omni-channel. They've brought in some consultants and done their own analysis. If you sell some type of omnichannel enablement—distribution and fulfillment, marketing, whatever—telling the buyer something they don't know could include firsthand knowledge you've gained through real-world deployments, such as the common pitfalls that caused delays.

Without divulging confidential information or giving away secrets, you can still provide companies with insights they wouldn't otherwise have access to about competitors' operations, project risk, or financial performance. You're working with many different customers. Bring that perspective with you to your meetings because it benefits your buyers and positions you as a valuable resource. Telling them how your solutions address their particular pain points with the competition—rather than just how many features a certain gadget includes—demonstrates insights into their business beyond simply what you're trying to sell.

Buyers are busy. They don't always have time to get the big picture on trends. You provide value by filling that need. If a seller doesn't have a perspective on what's happening in the industry or coming down the pike, all they have is their product knowledge—and executives don't care about your product knowledge. They have reports that can give them all the nitty-gritty around product details. Executives want information about the future of the industry and how to achieve their strategic goals, so your discussion should not be about product features but rather how you provide a solution that helps them compete within their industry while supporting their expected business outcomes.

INSIGHT-LED SELLING IN ACTION

Action: Tell an executive something they don't know

Purpose: Align your solutions with business benefits

Ideally, you will complete this action by applying it to one of your customers. But you can also go to www.InsightLedSelling.com for examples of common goals, strategies, and initiatives for select industries. Use the code INSIGHTSELLER to access the site.

1. Identify one of your customer's goals, strategies, and initiatives.

2. Based on these insights, what are some things you could tell the buyer *that they don't know that shows how your solution can help them achieve their goals, strategies, and initiatives?*

Deliver Business Outcomes

As shown in Figure 1-2, "What Do Executives Really Want from Your Solutions?," there are three factors that drive financial performance: *How fast are we growing? How profitable is the business? How well did we manage our assets?* A company's goals and strategies, and the individual lines of business's initiatives flow from the answers to these questions. What executives really want are solutions that align with those goals, strategies, and initiatives. Regardless of their department, those questions drive the conversation, and if you're not improving one of those three metrics in some tangible way, there's not going to be much interest in a solution because it won't be relevant.

Executives want your solutions to deliver business outcomes such as enhancing the customer and employee experience, improving time to market, mitigating risk, and improving agility and resiliency. These operational benefits lead to financial benefits.

You might say, for example, "I understand your goal is to increase profitability by improving manufacturing processes. Here's how our solutions have helped others in your industry improve their profitability by automating key manufacturing processes, specifically in the areas of labor and materials."

If you don't open the aperture to take a higher-level look at the three major buckets, you're just going to get into a price war. It's going to be all about price, price, price. Regardless of what you're selling, you need to take a bigger-picture view than price and explain how working with you will deliver expected business outcomes.

INSIGHT-LED SELLING IN ACTION

Action: Link your solution's financial performance to a customer's desired business outcomes

Purpose: Understand and better communicate how your solution delivers financial benefits

The three key Areas of Financial Performance are (1) revenue growth, (2) profitability, and (3) asset utilization.

- Which of these three areas of performance does your solution improve?

- Select one of these areas and create an elevator pitch explaining in nontechnical terms how your solution helps improve this area of performance for a customer.

Make Their Life Easier

At a conference Stephen attended as a speaker, one of the other speakers, a medical device company CEO, was asked what advice he'd give sellers. He said, "Don't show me anything too complex. If it's too complex, you haven't done your job, and I'm not going to spend much time thinking about it." Executives need you to give them enough information to assess whether the solution is a good idea. They don't want all the details; they want clarity. To

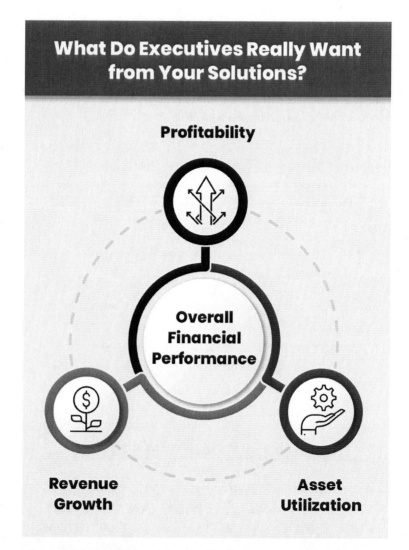

Figure 1-2. What Do Executives Really Want from Your Solutions? Their wants generally fall into these categories.

paraphrase Einstein, "Keep it simple but not too simple."

You have to respect executives' time and attention. They're very busy. Just because you're interested in something doesn't mean they are; you have to make your conversations relevant and explain what's in it for them. What you don't want is to become part of the burden for them. That's the fastest way to be passed down to an underling. Executives need someone they can trust to cut through the chaos and help them stand out from competitors. If you can persuade them of your ability to make their life easier, you'll keep their attention.

> *"I'll give sellers three pieces of advice:*
>
> *"Know the problem I'm trying to solve and how I've tried to solve it. Don't lose time in the conversation by making recommendations for avenues I've already explored.*
>
> *"Remember that it's all about my company's needs—not yours.*
>
> *"Be competent and knowledgeable about what you're selling and be flexible during our conversation. If your product isn't a perfect fit, be prepared to tell me how it can be adjusted to make it work."*
>
> **—DAWN GARIBALDI**, President, Amplify Strategy, and former Vice-President, Supply Chain, Fabric & Home Care–Asia, Procter & Gamble

STEP OUTSIDE YOUR COMFORT ZONE

You probably have go-to people in your accounts who help you along with your deals. Sometimes those are the only people you need. But it's easy to get comfortable and never take the next step of talking to executives in the company whose goals and strategies could benefit from your solution. That leaves opportunity on the table, because you could be bringing more value and, in effect, harvest more interest and support for a bigger deal.

At the same time, spending all your time with a single point of contact introduces risk because that person could move to a different role or even leave the company. Even if your current deal goes through, there may not be any commitment to the solution from others in the company. With no advocate, the odds of success won't be as good.

You need more than one relationship to see the big picture of what you can offer; you also need relationships to build and maintain trust, credibility, and influence. It's important to make yourself more relevant in the organization with insights into the broader context and how executives contribute to achieving a goal.

Your friend in the account may be acting as a gatekeeper. Yet, you know there are other stakeholders that you could and should be talking to. Don't be afraid to ask for an introduction. You are not putting your deal at risk; rather, you are expanding it to a wider audience whom you can help and who can help you.

Technology sellers, for example, used to be comfortable in the CIO's office. The problem is, the profile of the CIO is changing. A decade ago, CIOs tended to be technologists whose main responsibility was keeping the lights on. They were also focused on lowering the cost of IT. Now technology enables many other parts of the business. So instead of being a CTO or "Head of IT," the CIO is now an extension of the business. They're more of a business leader than a technology leader. CIOs today often come from other lines of business and they don't always have the technical depth required to "talk tech" with a technology seller. But sellers still have to talk to them. Trying to get the job done with someone a level or two below the CIO doesn't always cut it. You need to speak to the executive and you need to know their language.

Another challenge is talking to new buyers, which can happen for a variety of reasons, such as when your customer's company buys another company or when you create new products that solve problems for other lines of business. For example, we work with a wonderful supply management software company that has many bright sellers. They feel very comfortable talking to supply chain VPs about how a supply chain is a strategic weapon. Originally, they'd focused on warehouse management and how their solutions made them more efficient and the financial benefits. About five years ago, their new solution targeting retail offered to improve omnichannel management, grow the business, and better manage costs. Yes, they could pitch that to the VP of supply chain, but now marketing, store operations, and finance were involved in the decision too. They'd never worked with a CMO or VP of store operations, so they had to learn their key initiatives, understand how they measured success, and know how to talk to them in their language.

The buying landscape is constantly changing. Keeping up requires knowing your buyers—the real decision makers, who may be collaborating across departments—getting outside your comfort zone and learning to speak their language.

CORPORATE DECISION MAKING

Figure 1-3 shows the basic structure and characteristics of corporate decision making. As you move up or down the pyramid, what you talk about has to change.

At the top of the pyramid, executives have big-picture goals, strategies, and initiatives and they determine how to monitor a company's success. To maintain an attractive stock, they might aim to grow the company 5–10 percent per year. They'll be looking at market value, cash flow, return, earnings per share, and so on.

Moving down a level, the vice-president of Sales, for example, is focused on sales attainment, while operations will be focused on operating costs that impact profitability, and product development is looking at new product introduction. At the very bottom of the corporate decision-making pyramid, people tend to focus on shorter-term goals and items such as budget variances of operating expense and completing projects on time and within budget. They're concerned with what they need to get done that day, week, or quarter. They have particular metrics to hit, and your pitch about high-level strategy won't carry much weight with these people.

Most sales reps start having conversations at the bottom and strive to move to higher-level management and finally executives. Using a low-level conversation with a high-level executive won't work either. Depending on their place in the hierarchy, people's focuses and metrics are very different. You need to change your mindset to talk to the middle versus the top. Learn to tailor your conversation and you will see an impact on sales.

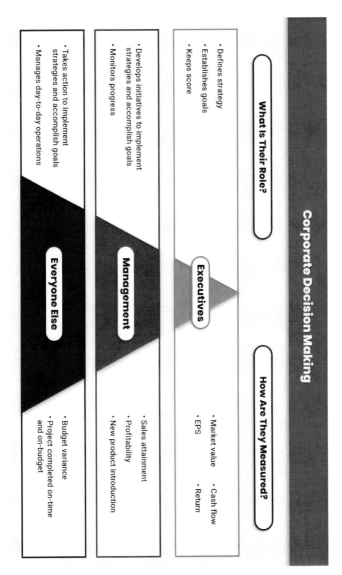

Figure 1-3. Corporate decision making is influenced by how people are measured, which varies between roles.

OPERATING AND FREE CASH FLOW

A COMPANY'S ABILITY TO GENERATE cash either currently and/or in the future is what gives it value. Two of the most referenced measures of cash flow are *Operating Cash Flow and Free Cash Flow.*

Operating Cash Flow is the cash generated from cash receipts from sales less all cash expenses such as operating expenses, interest, and taxes. **Free Cash Flow** is Operating Cash Flow less capital expenditures.

Companies focus on cash flow since it has all the levers of creating value such as how well revenue, operating expenses, taxes, and capital expenditures are managed.

Microsoft, for its fiscal year 2020, generated a little over **$60 billion** (yes, billion) in Operating Cash Flow and invested around **$15 billion** in capital expenditures, resulting in **$45 billion** in Free Cash Flow.

TRANSFORMING FROM VENDOR TO STRATEGIC PARTNER

"We want to partner with vendors that make us better. As a result of doing business together, we want them to do better too. That's the ideal relationship, but it requires the vendor taking the initiative to bring us something new, like information on what other companies are doing.

"In turn, we'll share our challenges and opportunities

*with them so they can create more value for us. That's the
preferred partnership we want with vendors, and those
partnerships are critically important."*

—STEVE CLANCEY, CIO, Georgia Pacific

There's a sort of hierarchy that classifies sellers, from the
point of view of the buyer:

1. Vendor

2. Preferred Supplier

3. Solution Provider

4. Trusted Advisor

5. Strategic Partner

To sell at the top, you have to transform the way executives view you. Instead of being seen as a vendor, strive to
become a strategic partner. Seventy-one percent of B2B
customers are willing to take their business elsewhere,
usually for a lower price, which is sad. This is a clue that most
sellers are indeed seen as simply vendors competing on price.
If you can go beyond being the vendor with the lowest price
and make an actual impact on the business by helping to grow
revenue, increase profits, or manage assets, executives will
value you as a preferred supplier, solution provider, trusted
advisor, and eventually, a strategic partner, and you will have
the opportunity to increase wallet share.

Of B2B clients, 71 percent are willing to take their business elsewhere, usually for a lower price.[4]

Executives have preconceived notions about suppliers, and you have to deepen your relationship to change their assumptions. Solution success and service are just table stakes. Aggressive selling doesn't do the job. Competence of your team is important but not the whole picture. Our experience has shown—and our interviews with executives have confirmed—*that executive buyers want business outcomes.* Aim to position yourself as a strategic partner at the executive level who measurably improves your customers' business, and watch your sales grow.

Typical vendors don't deeply understand the business, and they're rarely invited to meet with an executive. A step up from vendor is preferred supplier, whom an executive might see on an annual basis, then solution provider, whom they might see quarterly. A trusted advisor isn't a bad place to be. Your goal should be just above that, to being a strategic partner who, to the buyer, feels like an arm of their operation and part of the fabric of their company.

Making that transformation requires honest self-assessment. Who are you to your customers right now? How do you know? If you're stuck at the level of solution provider, you're probably not growing the account as much as you'd like. To deepen your relationship, you must hone your ability to articulate how your offerings align with their goals, strategies, initiatives, and ultimately, expected business outcomes. You must clearly explain, in executive terms, how much value you will bring with regard to increased profitability, growth, or asset utilization.

---

4   "Analytics and Advice for B2B Leaders," Gallup.com, 2017, https://www.gallup.com/analytics/267998/advice-for-b2b-leaders.aspx.

HOW TO COMMUNICATE WITH EXECUTIVES

Executives who give you a slot on their calendar expect you to respect their time. Do that by getting to the point, telling them how your solution aligns with their goals, and being up front about when your solution worked and when it didn't. You're not there to make a friend. You are there to solve a problem. Focus on that and you'll have their attention.

Get Straight to the Point

Executives talk to a lot of vendors, and their bullshit detector is always on. If you sound too salesy, they'll stop listening. Limit the pleasantries, skip the window dressing, and focus on the core messaging around the solution.

Tell Them Why It Matters

Don't lead with how much your solution costs or how much it will save them. That tactic can place you squarely in the "vendor" category, cost you credibility, and eliminate you and your solution from the running. Buyers often have a number in their head and need to hear more before adjusting those expectations.

Instead, lead with how your product fits with their goals and can help them implement their strategies and initiatives. That's what they care about, first and foremost. Demonstrate your familiarity with their situation and explain in nontechnical language how your solution aligns with their strategies. Come around to the cost and the financial benefits *after you've established that fit.*

TELL EXECUTIVES WHAT THEY WANT TO KNOW, NOT WHAT YOU WANT TO SAY

ONE OF OUR EXECUTIVE COACHES once ran Sales for a major telecommunications company. Later in his career, he was on the other side of the desk. The first few times sellers came in, he'd get irritated with them until he realized, "Oh, my God, that's what I sounded like."

Put yourself in your buyer's shoes and ask yourself, "What do they want to know?" and "What am I telling them?" How far apart are the answers?

Be Transparent

Buyers want sellers to be candid. They want them to be up front and not hide important information—both good and bad. Working with executives, we often hear comments such as, "Don't hide the problems or give me any surprises." These buyers tell us that vendors like to talk about all the great features of their product but fail to mention past issues or failures.

Talk about the business outcome benefits and successes,

and also tell them about the times implementations didn't turn out as planned. Don't blame those customers, though; instead, explain the lessons you learned and how you will leverage that knowledge for their implementation. Use your experience to show them how they can lower their own risk; being truthful about the potential challenges will build trust.

MAKE IT PERSONAL WITH EXECUTIVE COMPENSATION

The degree to which an executive is comfortable discussing executive compensation with you varies among executives and may be influenced by the strength of your relationship, but no matter whom you are talking to or how well you know them, you need to be aware of the details of executive compensation, how to find it, and most importantly, how to discuss it appropriately.

Executive decision making is obviously driven by company goals, but it's also driven by the executive buyer's individual compensation structure. If you know how your customer is compensated, you can use that information to get their attention. For example, if an executive is compensated based on profits, think about how your offerings can impact profits and mention that in your conversations. You don't have to be creepy and say, "I know you're compensated on profits, so you'll like what my solution can do," but don't be shy about clearly stating any benefit that impacts them directly.

In addition to salary, executives are usually compensated on annual and long-term incentives. Base salary is a given; that leaves incentives based on short- and long-term goals. Strategic goals tend to be esoteric, while annual compensation metrics goals are more tangible and easier to link to your solution. Annual compensation metrics vary a lot by industry and slightly within an industry. Figure 1-4, "Executive Compensation," shows some of the most common metrics.

Executive Compensation

Consumer Products	Banking
• Free Cash Flow • Earnings per Share	• Return on Equity • Cost-to-Income (Efficiency) Ratio • Net Income • Earnings per Share • Customer Satisfaction

Telecommunications	Oil and Gas
• Earning before Interest, Taxes, Depreciation, and Amortization (EBITDA) • Customer Experience • Employee Experience	• Cost per Barrel • Safety • Production

Figure 1-4. Executive compensation influences decision making and typically varies between industries.

COST-TO-INCOME (EFFICIENCY) RATIO

THE COST-TO-INCOME RATIO (CIR), ALSO known as the Efficiency Ratio, is a key driver of banks' and other financial institutions' financial performance. CIR is Noninterest Expenses expressed as a percentage of revenue. Noninterest expense includes items such as salaries and related expenses, IT services, premises and equipment, professional fees, and regulatory fees. For large banks in North America, the CIR averages around **60 percent**, which means noninterest expenses absorb around $0.60 for each $1.00 in revenue. By comparison, the better performers' CIR is closer to **55 percent**.

Banks typically are focused on improving the CIR by better managing all its components.

EARNINGS BEFORE INTEREST, TAXES, DEPRECIATION, AND AMORTIZATION (EBITDA)

EBITDA IS A COMMONLY USED measure of profits for companies in capital-intensive industries such as industrial manufacturing, metals, and mining. EBITDA is revenue less direct costs such as materials, labor, and overhead; and indirect costs such as sales and marketing, IT, and product development. Caterpillar, for example, for its latest twelve months at the time of the writing of this book, had around **$8.5 billion** in EBITDA, which was **$43.7 billion** in revenue less approximately

$35.2 billion in direct and indirect costs. Companies use EBITDA because it helps people focus on what they have the most control over in the near term.

EBITDA is often expressed as a percentage of revenue to assess changes in EBITDA over time and compare it to other companies. This is called the EBITDA Margin. The average **EBITDA Margin** for industrial Machinery and Equipment manufacturers in Europe is around **13 percent** and **17 percent** for better performers.

How to Find Compensation Data

Executive compensation isn't "insider information"—it's often in the public domain. Publicly traded companies in the United States include that information in their definitive proxy statement, also known as SEC Form DEF 14A. Outside the United States, it's in a company's annual report in the section titled "Remuneration" or "Compensation." Businesses post these online, so just go to the company's website and look under tabs such as "Investor Relations" and "Financial Statements." Bear in mind that there are cultural nuances in the accuracy of data from one country to the next. North American and European countries tend to be more transparent about this information, while countries in other regions of the world, such as Asia, tend to generalize the data.

How to Talk about It
(without Being Creepy)

There's a right and a wrong way to introduce compensation into your conversations, illustrated in Figure 1-5. See if you can tell the difference:

"Ms. Raymond, I know you made two and a half million dollars last year, but wouldn't it be nice to hit your metrics on net income and return on equity? I can help you with those, as well as your customer satisfaction and loyalty initiatives. Buy from me, and you'll meet your annual goals, collect on your compensation package, and finally be able to afford to take Mr. Raymond—and those adorable Raymond children, Moe, Larry, and little Curly Joe—on that trip around the world!"

versus

"Ms. Raymond, our company aims to help you achieve your goal of getting your product to market faster, which will improve financial performance in areas such as net income, return on equity, and risk and strategic initiatives."

In the second example, you don't sound like a stalker, but you've communicated benefits that will resonate with the buyer on a personal level.

The caveat to this is that you should always consider your relationship with the buyer. If this is your first conversation, obviously lean heavily toward "not creepy." But if you've talked to them before and they trust you, you actually can stretch the boundaries by speaking specifically to their compensation without making them uncomfortable. At least one executive buyer we interviewed told us they are completely comfortable with those conversations:

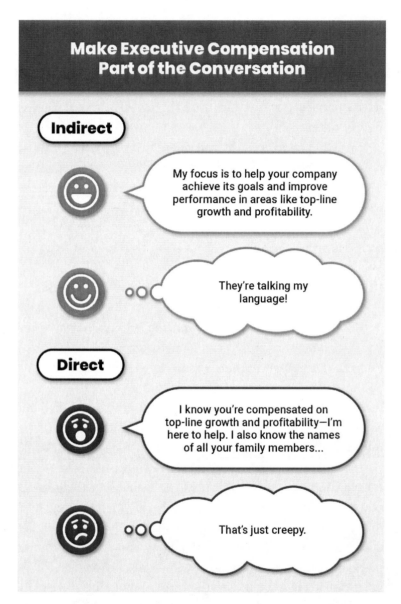

Figure 1-5. Make Executive Compensation Part of the Conversation—but do it without being creepy.

"I don't mind sellers knowing how I'm measured. We're a public company and they can find that information in our proxy statement. Executives are often measured on return on assets and a few other things, and if a seller tells me, 'I understand that this is how you're measured, and this is how I can help you with that,' and they can actually prove it, they have my attention. Some people don't like to talk about executive compensation, but I view it as, 'Okay, they did their research.' That's not a bad thing."

—CFO of a community bank

HOW EXECUTIVE COMPENSATION IMPACTS THE ORGANIZATION

Imagine you're selling logistics solutions and calling a warehouse manager or selling automation solutions and calling an individual plant. Although it's interesting to know how executives are compensated, those likely won't be the relevant metrics to the person you're talking to at a warehouse or plant. Their compensation will operate differently. So why is executive compensation relevant in that case? Think about how executive compensation impacts the organization, shown in Figure 1-6.

Let's take a large retail chain example. The highest level, the "executives," includes the CEO, CFO, and senior VPs of major geographical operations. They occupy the tippy top and get compensated on sales and profits. They focus not only on yearly sales but also on clearing a decent profit on those sales (Operating Income).

OPERATING INCOME
(PROFIT)

OPERATING INCOME, WHICH IS ALSO known as **Operating Profit**, is one of the most widely used measures of profits. Operating Income is revenue less direct and indirect costs and unlike EBITDA, it also takes out depreciation and amortization. Operating Income is EBITDA less depreciation and amortization. Going back to the Caterpillar example, Operating Income was around **$6.0 billion**, which is the **$8.5 billion** in EBITDA less **$2.5 billion** in depreciation and amortization. Companies often use Operating Income because it helps people focus on all the elements of profits.

Operating Income is often expressed as a percentage of revenue, which is referred to as **Operating Income Margin.** The average Operating Income Margin for large consumer products companies in South America is around 10 percent and for better performers, **12 percent.**

If we go down a level, we start getting into the people at the top of the more functional areas, such as the vice-presidents of supply chain management, merchandising, and store operations. They look at total logistics cost, in the case of supply chain management, because that impacts Operating Income. Merchandising—selecting the merchandise—impacts sales as well. The merchandising VP wants to know the sell-through rate, the profit margin, and whether there were a lot of markdowns, impacting both sales and Operating Income. Then the VP managing all the thousands of stores will have responsibility for how productive those stores are, looking at both sales and operating costs.

Finally, we get to everyone else. This group includes individual store managers, individual Distribution and Logistics managers, the regional director of HR, and so on. They take the high-level metrics and break them into smaller pieces.

A store manager would look at individual store sales and the profit on those sales, as well as labor costs and theft rate. Even though they're not managing the huge corporation, they're managing a good-sized enterprise. They hear from higher-ups every week about how actual sales compare to forecast and about having overtime when they weren't supposed to.

Like the store manager, the distribution manager aligns with the executives' interests by keeping track of labor costs, maintenance costs, overtime, delivery performance, and the like. If they're supposed to ship online orders next day, what percentage of those shipments actually go out on time without errors or damage? That's what they care about. If you're talking to the distribution manager, you won't necessarily look at Operating Income because distribution centers are not considered profit centers. However, you'll look at components that will eventually drive Operating Income.

The director of HR will focus on issues such as labor turnover. Higher turnover means spending more on acquiring talent and having a less experienced workforce. As employees move up the experience curve, they become more effective in terms of costs and helping customers make purchases, so there's a sales component.

The point here is even if you're not talking to the top executives, having insight into executive's incentives will help you break down how the various tasks and Key Performance Indicators serve the overall strategy.

SUMMARY

Insights into how executives think and what they want from your solution will help you move from vendor to trusted advisor and, eventually, strategic partner. Learn to speak their language and tailor it to others' roles too.

Buyers want you to talk to them not only in terms of their key metrics but also in the context of their industry. It doesn't work to use a manufacturing pitch for someone not in manufacturing. You don't have to be an industry expert, but make sure you know what's going on in that sector—the technology and business trends, as well as some of the risks. Once you've gotten into the mindset of an executive, it's time to gather key insights on their industry.

EXECUTIVE INSIGHTS BEST PRACTICES

Following these Insight-Led Selling best practices will help you avoid being seen as a vendor who's easily dismissed by top buying executives, and instead valued as a partner who can help them reach their goals.

- **Do your research.** Have clear insights into your customer's business, what drives it, their key problems, and their expected business outcomes.

- **Don't start out by talking about your product, technology, features, or functions.** This is like a hammer looking for a nail. Executives have no time or interest unless you start with their needs. Instead, grab your customer's attention by focusing on a key need or business driver that can benefit from your offering. Make sure your solution can produce real business outcomes by improving operational and financial performance around this driver and talk about the impact before you talk about your product.

- **Executive compensation starts at the top level.** If it's important in the C-suite, similar compensation metrics will flow downhill to other levels of the organization. Tie your solution to key bonus metrics, but instead of directly talking about the buyer's incentives, simply mention how your solution drives key metrics and let the executive link this to their bonus.

- **Tell the customer something they don't already know.** Go beyond tech and specs and help them solve a problem.

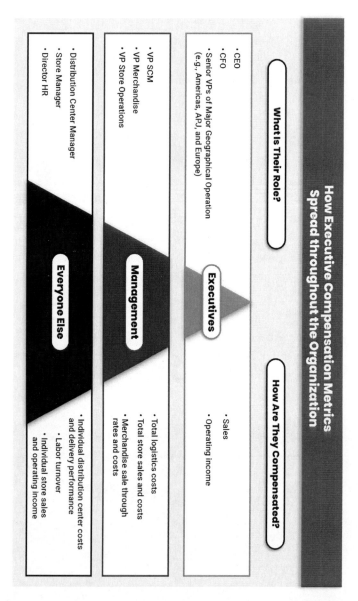

Figure 1-6. How Executive Compensation Metrics Spread throughout the Organization illustrates how compensation often relies on a person's role.

2

INDUSTRY INSIGHTS

"I want a seller to have deep knowledge and demonstrated capability in my industry. Show me where you've done this before. Bring me references so I can call them. I need to be confident that this seller has a solid track record of success in the work they're proposing."

—STEVE CLANCEY,

CIO, Georgia Pacific

One day Andrea, a software salesperson and one of our clients, came to us for help. She was struggling with one of her customers, a bank. There was a large deal on the table that she couldn't close, and she didn't understand why. We asked Andrea how she was presenting the solution, and everything she said made sense, but the elements she addressed and terminology she used were so generic that she wasn't breaking through to the decision makers. They were hearing the same words every other salesperson who stepped into their offices used: "Here's how we can help you manage your business better, faster, cheaper, etc." Okay, but what does that *mean*? Without specifics, as far as the bank was concerned, she had no credibility.

Although Andrea understood the bank's needs and how her solution addressed them, she didn't understand the banking industry's core elements nor have the right words to discuss them. We showed her what she *should* be talking about, in banking terms the decision makers would understand. Most importantly, we taught her about the banking industry's core metric—Cost-to-Income Ratio.

If you've ever worked with banks, you've probably heard the term "cost-to-income (efficiency) ratio," an important metric for financial institutions and one that a buyer in that industry expects their sellers to know. Armed with this new industry knowledge, Andrea got another meeting with the bank, talked to them about the potential impact of her solution on their Efficiency Ratio, and closed the deal.

Knowing industry insights—such as how your customer's industry measures performance—provides many advantages:

- Allows you to think more broadly about the impact of your customer's issues and the potential value of your solution

- Gains trust with your customer, so they are more willing to share information with you about their priorities

- Better prepares you to offer a solution that delivers better business outcomes

INDUSTRY ESSENTIALS

"A seller doesn't have to know everything I know about my business or my industry, but they should know a good portion of what I know. And they must understand the competitive landscape. They should know my strengths and my problems—and those of my competitors. That's how they can sell to me: by understanding where I'm weak and someone else is strong, and helping me to close that gap."

—KEN MAY, former CEO, Top Golf and former Chief Operating Officer, Krispy Kreme Doughnuts

Common corporate goals such as profitability exist across all industries. However, within each industry there exist metrics, measures, and goals that are somewhat unique to that industry. Without knowing an industry's essentials—what actually *matters* to the decision makers at companies within the industry—you cannot align your team, set up a strategy, or bring the right resources to your customers at the right time. You might be doing just enough to keep the business, or maybe they're working with you because of the relationship you've built, but you are ripe for losing that account to the first salesperson who steps in and shows the decision maker how they can make a difference in what truly matters to executive buyers. In banking, it's Efficiency Ratio. In brick-and-mortar retail, it's revenue per square foot and how to combat Amazon and other online resellers to increase revenue.

Knowing your customer's industry essentials helps you understand why a customer is focused on certain initiatives that to an uninformed vendor might seem counterintuitive. For example, a well-managed business might still see falling profit margins, which on paper, looks bad. Yet, instead of focusing on growth, which you would typically expect, they are shifting their goals to managing costs to counteract the situation. Without insight into the logic behind their decision, you wouldn't understand why managing costs is essential for the company.

Insights into an industry's essentials gets you further in the door. It shows the customer you know their business, even though, technically, you're not in their business. You have a wider, deeper perspective of the industry and understand their situation within the context of that industry, and that immediately puts you ahead of the game.

Gaining industry insight comprises "walking the walk" with a clear understanding of the essentials and "talking the talk" with the right vocabulary—financial fluency around them. Buyers expect you to know their industry and be able to talk about it.

BE AWARE OF SHIFTS IN INDUSTRY ESSENTIALS

INDUSTRY ESSENTIALS ARE RELATIVELY STATIC over time, but major events like 9/11 or financial downturns such as the Great Recession that began in 2007 can quickly shift metrics and even make them obsolete. The COVID-19 pandemic impacted the oil and gas industry, which incurred significant losses in 2020. Being efficient isn't enough when the demand for a product evaporates. A company that was spending capital expenditure on building new rigs, fracking, drilling, and trying to become the number one oil producer in the universe had to change course. Their focus moved to cutting costs to remain solvent.

Likewise, the airlines—even the best ones—were deeply affected during this time because no matter how stellar their service records, people weren't getting on planes. In these instances, you can see how an industry's metrics might change due to factors beyond their control. A salesperson has to be aware of these changes before they walk into a sales call. Approaching the company with a solution focused on growth over cost cutting wouldn't get a seller very far.

Inversely, the pandemic caused some industries to thrive—Zoom, for example, suddenly blew up when people had to work from home to meet social distancing requirements. You can bet their metrics changed too.

Today, consumers of retail and consumer products are unwilling to wait three days for a delivery. They want it tomorrow or in two days max. As a result, companies in these industries are moving their distribution centers much closer to the customer, using what is called distributive logistics. Instead of having just a few big centers, they have either many smaller warehouses, or they cohabitate with other businesses or have co-locations with third parties.

If you don't know the changes in the industry, you won't have insight into the focus of each line of business buyer within a particular industry. You could meet with a buyer and talk to them about cost, not knowing that cost isn't even on their top-ten list of concerns. It may still be important but not important enough for the buyer to give you their time. Know the industry essentials and be aware of the changes so you can tailor your solution and your conversation accordingly.

TELL BUYERS SOMETHING THEY DON'T KNOW

As a seller who talks to dozens of customers every year, you have a distinct advantage over your buyers, who don't have that same opportunity. You know what other companies are doing and can identify current risks and trends. You also know how other companies are mitigating risks and capitalizing on trends because you are helping them do just that. This insight establishes you as a credible source of information and guidance because you can tell a customer something they don't already know that most applies to their business too, based on your research and real-world experience.

Buyers often don't have the same information you have because they don't talk to as many people as you do. We worked with a company that helps customers develop apps more quickly and cheaply. It operated almost exclusively in the IT area and was well received. We pointed out the IT group for this company's customers would have to go get funding and asked how many of these apps ultimately drive increased revenue. The answer was "a lot."

We noted that if the company gets development done in a third of the time and there are revenue benefits to the solution, then it's not just about cost savings. They had a big light bulb moment: when seeking funding, they should work with the IT group to go to the marketing and the sales groups, ask if they can spare any budget, and explain how much of an increase in revenue the investment could drive. Their primary contact was IT, but IT had not thought about the revenue benefits of faster development. So by virtue of helping the account team think about their solution in a different way, we helped them to then communicate a new, financially focused perspective to the customer: they were able to tell their customer something they didn't know.

SEVEN STEPS FOR GETTING TO KNOW YOUR CUSTOMER'S INDUSTRY

Figure 2-1, "Knowing Your Customer's Industry Key Elements," illustrates our proven seven-step process for getting to know a customer's industry. Briefly, here are descriptions of each step. We'll walk you through an example shortly so you understand how you can use these steps in a real-world situation. It is important to note this is a group activity: include members such as Sales and Marketing, and industry experts. It can be a lot of work, but the benefits are significant. The end result is a playbook that can be used for developing marketing collateral and for working with individual customers.

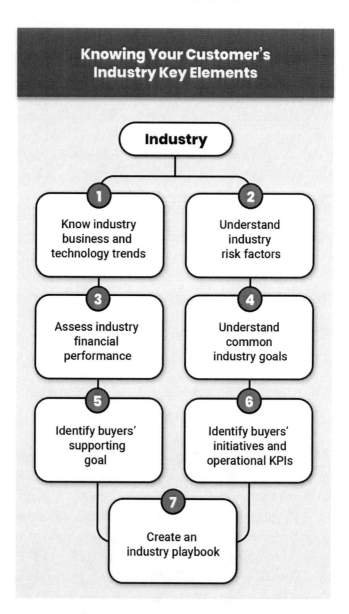

Figure 2-1. Knowing your customer's industry's key elements is critical to providing a solution that matters to the buyer.

Step 1: Start with business and technology trends. Knowing the industry's business and technology trends, consider how your solution helps the customer leverage or mitigate the impact of these trends.

Step 2: Then understand the industry's common risks. Common risks exist within each industry. Determine which of these operational, customer, and economic risks affect your customer.

Step 3: Assess industry financial performance. The industry in which a company competes is one of the most important drivers of its financial performance. Identify trends in performance and factors causing those trends. Then see how your customer compares with industry averages.

Step 4: Learn the common industry goals and strategies. Learning common industry goals and strategies provides insight into those of your customers and their competitors. Companies react to common goals differently, and your research and experiences with many companies provide a breadth of knowledge. Your customers are interested in hearing what other businesses are doing. You can make recommendations based on that knowledge and perhaps tell buyers something they didn't know that could help guide their strategies and better achieve their goals.

Step 5: Identify buyers' supporting goals and strategies. The next step is to identify those buyers that are supporting the common industry goals and strategies. This helps you not only better understand your current buyers but also helps identify new buyers. In Chapter 3, we explore this in more detail for individual company goals and strategies.

Step 6: Identify buyers' initiatives and Operational KPIs. Knowing the buyers that support the common industry goals and strategies, the next step is to identify their supporting initiatives and the Operational Key Performance Indicators (KPIs) they use to measure success. This helps you develop better value statements about how your solutions deliver business outcomes and the financial benefits. In Chapter 3, we explore buyers' initiatives and KPIs in more detail.

Step 7: Create a playbook. Creating a scalable industry playbook that you can apply to individual accounts helps tie all the pieces together so you can tell the story in a way that resonates with the buyer and is easy to understand without being overwhelming. If you have a knowledge management person in your organization, you can hand off the documentation, organization, and updating of the playbook to them, with the insight that Sales and Marketing and others should continue to contribute new information as it becomes available.

Applying the Seven Steps:
Consumer Products Example

"Larger companies struggle with innovation, so they value outside sources that bring them new ideas. A vendor who invests time to learn about a company's industry—its current risks, trends, and needs—and who knows the customer well enough to leverage their industry knowledge and bring innovation to them has something of real value to offer that customer."

—BILL CORTNER, President, Cortner Consulting, LLC, former Director, Procter & Gamble Purchases, and VP, J.M. Smucker Company

Now that we've reviewed the seven steps for getting to know your customer's industry, let's apply those steps to a real industry, in this example, consumer products. Even if you don't sell into this particular industry, these instructions will provide a framework for selling into your own customers' industries.

STEP 1: KNOW BUSINESS AND TECHNOLOGY TRENDS

Knowing an industry's business and technology trends offers the seller unique benefits:

- Helps you better understand how your solutions can help your customers embrace positive trends and address the negative ones

- Provides a framework for you to assess trends that already have your customer's focus and identify potential gaps

- Provides a potential opportunity to tell buyers something they don't know about managing trends

Business Trends

Companies craft goals and strategies that respond to business trends at a macro level. They prioritize the most important issues and focus on how to manage them. They also look at how their competitors manage them. Some trends are opportunities (positive), while others are setbacks (negative).

Examples of the consumer products industry trends are shown in Figure 2-2.

> *"When a seller starts thinking that their customer has all of the answers, that's when they're in trouble. I love learning something I don't know. It's very powerful when a seller says, 'I can't specifically say the customer's name, but another customer in your industry did this.'*
>
> *"Industry knowledge builds great credibility. The seller doesn't even have to know all the specifics of the problem I'm trying to solve, because it's often going to be similar to the problems other companies in the industry are trying to solve too. We all tend to have the same challenges.*
>
> *"If a seller doesn't offer any industry knowledge, I ask them, 'You all do a lot of work in my industry; what are the great things that other companies are doing that we are missing?'"*
>
> **—CANDY CONWAY,** former VP Global Operations, AT&T

Companies are constantly looking at business trends within their industries and adjusting their goals and strategies accordingly. A current trend in consumer products businesses is to get closer to the customer by bypassing resellers and selling directly to the consumer. Another current business trend is subscription selling, such as Gillette's Shave Club. The advantage of selling by subscription is that it creates repeat customers and reduces acquisition costs. Then the company can pass that savings on to the customer with lower prices.

Industry Trends: Consumer Products

Business Trends

- Retail operating model shift
- Consumer preferences evolving
- Product development
- Operational excellence
- Customer and partner support
- Strategic partnerships and investments
- Market disruptions

Tech Trends

- Digital technology
- Data and analytics
- Omnichannel
- Technology-enabled innovations
- Cybersecurity
- Cloud platform

Figure 2-2. Industry Trends: Consumer Products shows some common business and tech trends in the consumer products industry.

Another common business trend in this industry is getting the attention of millennials. Brands such as Betty Crocker and Campbell's soup may still attract boomers, but they don't resonate with younger people. With the over-fifty audience aging out, companies that have been around for generations have had to find new ways to tap into a new market. Similarly, brands such as Coca-Cola and Pepsi have come up against a generation more interested in vitamin waters and juices than sugary, carbonated drinks, and those brands have lost their luster.

Technology Trends

Digital technology and online banking revolutionized the banking industry. Social media changed how sales and marketing are done. And these technologies aren't static—they're still changing all the time. Data analytics, omnichannel, robotics, and AI are all technology trends that are evolving quickly, affecting how companies do business.

For any given sector, consider which business trends are taking shape and how your customers can leverage technology trends to meet the new challenges and accomplish their goals. How can your solution help them accelerate by taking advantage of trends, or better respond to trends that are going against them? The business landscape is always changing; technology continues to evolve. Help your customers look at their technology investments as a means to accelerating their ability to meet and leverage business trends to their benefit.

Step 2: Understand Industry Risk Factors

Growing the business and managing expenses are important, but publicly traded companies are required to devolve what they see as risks to the business so they must scan for threats. As a seller, you do not need to know every possible risk to your customers in their industry, but you should understand the major ones. The main areas of concern appear in companies' annual reports. Publicly traded companies have to divulge that information to investors, which benefits your research. If you're working with a private company, you can still get a sense of risk based on what similar publicly traded companies report and by observing the industry landscape. Consider the following benefits of understanding industry risk factors:

- Provides a framework to show the benefits of your solutions

- Helps compare the risks your customer's executives are focused on with those of the industry

- Offers the potential opportunity to tell executives something they don't know about managing risks

Rather than asking customers what's bothering them, put in the legwork to research the business environment and come up with hypotheses and potential solutions in advance. People used to do a lot of question-based selling, but you shouldn't ask a customer what you can discover yourself. In other words, don't risk appearing out of touch—do your homework. When you come in with a targeted plan and curiosity that shows you're thoughtful and knowledgeable, customers will often offer up their strategy deck in response, at which point you'll have exactly what you need to propose the best solutions. Keep in mind that not all factors are negative—you can also anticipate positives (just ask Elon Musk). With the right approach, you can sometimes transform a risk into an opportunity.

Risks tend to fall within three categories: operational risk, customer risk, and economic risk. Figure 2-3 illustrates the most common industry risk factors in the consumer products industry, but many of these risks exist across other industries as well.

Operational Risk

Operational risks and unsuccessful strategy initiatives can hamper your customers' goals. Companies have a lot of control, though not total, over operational risk. The business meltdown in 2020 showed the importance of having built-in, fast-and-easy-to-implement responses to disruptions to the supply chain. Many companies struggled to get parts and supplies necessary for manufacturing. Employment rates and surplus or shortage of skilled labor also affect the industry.

It's important to understand your customer's specific concerns in this area because these issues are top of mind for senior leadership. They can only think about so many things. If one of the major risks is disruption to the supply chain or retaining qualified personnel, then you can pitch your offerings with regard to those challenges.

From an operational risk standpoint, a trusted advisor (as

Industry Risk Factors: Consumer Products

Operational Risk

- Unsuccessful strategic initiatives
- Disruption in supply chain
- Retention of qualified personnel
- Failure to keep pace with technological advances
- Cyberattacks, security, and data breaches

Customer Risk

- Adapt to changing consumer trends
- Failure to deliver innovative products
- Impact of technology changes
- Regulatory compliance
- Safety risks

Economic Risk

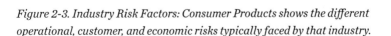

- Uncertain/weakening economic conditions
- Fluctuations in prices
- Trade partnerships
- Competition
- Intellectual property protections
- Expansion and development in new markets
- Global trade policies

Figure 2-3. Industry Risk Factors: Consumer Products shows the different operational, customer, and economic risks typically faced by that industry.

opposed to a mere vendor) looks at what a customer should be controlling. This might include items such as what the personnel situation looks like and whether there's the ability to invest in technology. Failure to keep pace with technological advances, including internet security, represents a risk. Failure to prepare for a critical employee who's hard to replace, such as an IT manager, is a risk.

These operational risks are common in other industries as well. In banking, for example, a benchmarking exercise showed that a major US bank had much less of an investment in technology than its competitors. At the time, the bank's leaders were proud of that fact. They actually touted their low-single-digit technology investment when other banks were investing two or three times as much. Then the company got hacked. Only then did they realize an insufficient investment in technology had exposed them to that risk. Cyberattacks represent a major risk across all industries. Companies control their own security, so if someone hacks them, it happens on their watch and falls within their sphere of control.

Anticipate problems and offer solutions before the customer faces a crisis. Imagine cementing your value with a customer by tailoring *preventive solutions* rather than reacting to mitigate crises they've already endured. Thinking through your customer's unique situation and coming to them with a great idea goes above and beyond what most of your competitors are doing.

Customer Risk

Like operational risks, companies also have a lot of control over customer risks. Even though customers want what they want and you can't impose preferences, you can *stay ahead of the curve.* Companies can and should anticipate and respond to changes in consumer behavior.

Companies have to maintain current customers and attract new ones, and as a seller, you should know whether your customers are keeping up with the competition in this area. Walmart, for example, has invested heavily in online to remain competitive. Similarly, from a product standpoint, if the grocer Publix had not switched over to healthier, organic brands, it would have missed that trend and lost sales.

Shifting delivery models is another example of a customer trend that can be seen as a risk or explored as an opportunity. When customers started ordering more groceries online for delivery to their homes, stores that didn't offer that option missed out.

Younger customers tend to have more social media fluency than older ones, which affects their clothing purchases. While a mature man or woman might focus on investing in lasting, classic pieces for their wardrobe, a younger person might go for cheaper, off-brand clothing because they don't want to repeat outfits in their Instagram feeds. Clothing used to last a long time, but some newer brands seem to deteriorate in an instant; they're not made to last because so many people keep trading up.

As automated vehicles become more prevalent and accidents decrease, customers will likely be paying lower rates. Auto insurance companies will have to consider how to continue making a good profit. Cars in general have a shifting market, too, as a lot of younger people don't need to own a vehicle if they live in an urban area with public transit or have access to Uber or Lyft.

Customer risks and opportunities abound, and each industry has its own considerations. What matters to your customers are their customers. Think about your customer but also about their customers. Many sellers don't make that connection.

Economic Risk

Economic risk typically involves factors outside of your customer's control. Economic conditions, material prices, and competitor reach shift over time. You may not be able to help your customer with some aspects of economic risk, but there could be ways to help them mitigate the impact.

In the past, companies leveraged technology to reduce costs, then put the savings back into developing new products or retaining more qualified personnel. By now, though, most of that low-hanging fruit has been picked. To deal with economic risk, they need to get smarter and more creative with their cost cutting, increased efficiency strategies. Timelines are shrinking too. Your buyer doesn't always have time to react as quickly as they'd like to. As a seller, it's important to understand most customers don't want to wait eighteen months to get their money back. Can you help them break even in six months instead? Anytime there's a recession, buyers want to speed up the process.

As mentioned earlier, economic risks affect customer risks. People who are in fear of losing their jobs think twice about buying premium brands. During recessions, customers tend to avoid larger expenditures and some shift their spending to other categories.

Multiple economic factors interact to drive trends and

initiate risks and opportunities. Companies want to know how to keep up with the spikes and shifts that create significant changes in demand for their products. Help them get there, but don't always be selling either. Sometimes as a seller, it's your job to maintain the account and assist the buyer with their day-to-day challenges.

STEP 3: ASSESS INDUSTRY FINANCIAL PERFORMANCE

Knowing your customer's industry performance provides the following benefits, to name a few:

- Builds credibility, since executive buyers expect you to know their industry with financial performance being one of the most important factors

- Helps create a viewpoint of where your solutions add the greatest value in the industry

- Provides perspective on your customer's relative performance, which helps identify potential areas of opportunity

Financial Drivers

It's hard to swim upstream in a negative economic context. Regardless of the economic situation, though, it's important to understand how your customer's individual financial performance compares to that of the industry. You might notice, for example, that the company's revenue has trended upward over the last five years while profitability has declined. You can ask about pricing and product mix, as well as explaining what you've seen other companies do to boost their overall growth as their margins have dropped.

Such numbers vary by company as well as by industry. Some industries simply have better margins and more to spend. For example, overall industry profitability for tech is significantly higher than for grocery.

Having this knowledge as a seller builds your credibility. You should be motivated to identify the higher performers in your industry and figure out what makes them tick because doing so arms you with knowledge to share with your customer, establishing your value. You want to help push your customers from the middle of the pack to a place among the better performers. If you're working with a company that's a laggard, it's important to figure out what they're doing or failing to do that's keeping them from even being average.

Figure 2-4, "Financial Drivers Map: Goods and Services Companies," shows what we call a Financial Drivers Map for product companies such as manufacturing, wholesale distribution, retail, and telecommunications. It provides a useful framework for understanding an industry's performance and where your solutions provide the greatest financial benefits. The appendix at the end of this book includes examples of Financial Drivers Maps for banking and insurance. In this section, we explore two of the most important drivers of financial performance—revenue growth and profitability. Assessing these two areas of industry performance and applying those learnings to sales provides a process to apply to other Areas of Financial Performance.

As you assess your customer's industry and, for that matter, your customer's performance, keep in mind the following:

- Companies seldom have exactly the same mix of products, strategies, business model, and so forth. So some differences in performance are almost always due to what we call unique company factors. This means differences in performance are explained in part by these unique company factors. Not all the differences represent opportunities for improvement. But experience does suggest where there are differences, there are some opportunities.

- Do not just focus on a single area of financial performance since many of the areas are connected operationally or by business strategy. You need to look at the bigger picture. For example, the strategy may be to grow market share by having lower prices and/or providing services that enhance the customer experience. This hopefully results in more revenue and growth but will lower profitability. Think of Amazon in the early days. Utilities provide a good example of how areas of performance are connected operationally. Utilities are very capital intensive, having to invest billions in generation, transmission, and distribution assets to generate revenue. Compared to other industries, utilities invest much more in assets to generate revenue. We will see that utilities also tend to have one of the highest profit margins across industries. Focusing just on their high profitability and not the bigger picture you may think, *"I knew it. I pay way too much in utilities bill...Their rates are too high. I'm getting screwed."* You may feel that way, but utilities need higher profitability to earn a competitive return on the billions they invest in assets to provide power to your home and business.

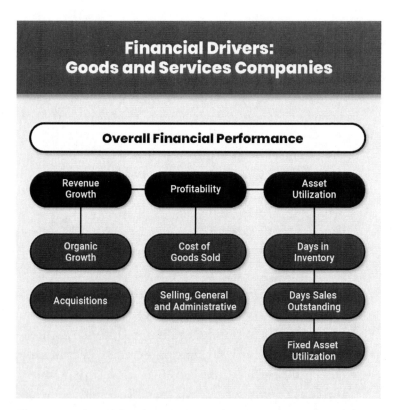

Figure 2-4. Financial Drivers Map: Goods and Services Companies.

Revenue Growth

When looking at financial performance, it all starts with revenue growth. Revenue growth is the year-over-year or quarter-over-quarter percentage change in revenue. Companies with higher growth tend to have a higher market valuation and have greater access to funds. Revenue growth is so important that it is commonly used as a part of executive compensation.

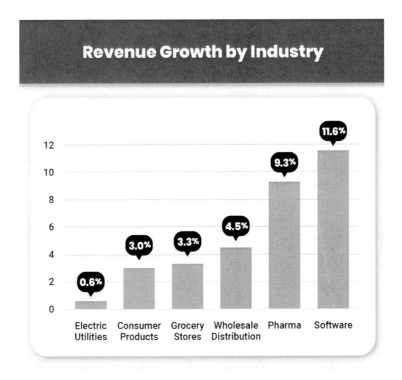

Figure 2-5. Five-year average revenue growth for 2015–2019 varies significantly by industry. Source: FinListics ClientIQ.

Revenue growth at an industry level is driven by factors such as overall demand, innovation, and how competitive and mature the market is. It can vary significantly by industry. Figure 2-5 shows average annual revenue growth for selected industries headquartered in North America with $1 billion or more in annual revenue. Software has one of the highest industry growth rates of around 12 percent. Software is a very competitive industry but also very innovative, providing offerings that help companies perform better while enhancing the lives of individuals.

The grocery industry is much lower at just a little over 3 percent. Why? Think about it. It's based on consumption. So unless enough people decide to change their caloric intake, it's going to grow at about the same rate as population growth with some growth for inflation. Take the United States as an example. Population growth in recent years has been around 0.6 percent and inflation, around 2 percent. It's not surprising, then, that the average industry growth rate for groceries is approximately 3 percent.

Does this mean you should focus your solutions only on industries with the highest growth rate? Not at all. An industry's growth rate is just a dimension of financial performance. For example, Figure 2-5 shows that electric utilities has the lowest average growth of less than 1 percent. Sounds kind of boring. But you will see shortly it has one of the highest levels of profitability. Not so boring now.

It's important to know the average revenue growth for your customer's industry, but it is also insightful to see how growth has changed over time and how the average annual growth compares to the better performers. Again, knowing this helps

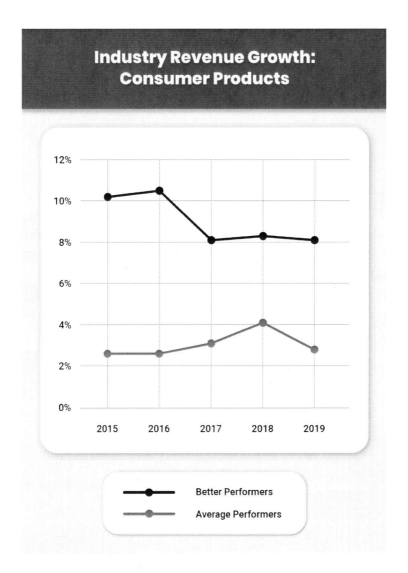

Figure 2-6. Industry revenue growth for consumer products companies headquartered in North America with over $1 billion in revenue, 2015–2019. Source: FinListics ClientIQ.

build credibility and also provides valuable benchmarks to compare your customer's performance. We know, having worked with many companies like your customers over the years, that benchmarking performance to the industry is very common. Knowing how your customer compares to the industry helps put you on the same page as company executives and provides an excellent opportunity to tell buyers something they don't know, such as what the better performers are doing differently.

Figure 2-6, "Industry Revenue Growth: Consumer Products," shows revenue growth over time for the consumer products industry for North American companies with over $1 billion in revenue. It shows the average and better performers. The average has grown over time at around 3 percent where the better performers have grown on average three times higher at around 9 percent!

It is important to know what the better performers are doing differently since you will find that most of your customers will be closer to the industry average. Why is this? Don't you remember from your statistics class the Law of Larger Numbers? You don't? That's all right; it just says that the more companies you engage with, the closer their performance will be closer to the average performance.

What might the better performers be doing differently? Do they tend to make more acquisitions to boost revenue? Are they leveraging business and technology trends for revenue growth such as omnichannel, digital marketing, sales force automation, and faster time to market for new products better and more quickly? You'd obviously want to know the answers from the perspective of what your solution delivers. Ideally, some of the companies in the better performers group are your customers. You could share with your other customer observations on what you see them doing differently. (Nothing confidential, of course.) Maybe some of the better performers in revenue growth have a different pricing strategy that sacrifices profitability for growth. Think of market disruptors who often want first to prove their business model can generate revenue and then work on the path to profitability.

Wait, what if some of your customers are already better performers? What do you tell them? They want insights into how to remain better performers. Executives know it's hard to stay at the top. Lots of companies are either trying to copy what the better performers are doing or leapfrog them.

We have conducted this type of analysis many times. What we find is most companies have a pretty good idea of the industry's average performance and how they compare. What they seem most interested in are the better performers. What are they doing differently? What strategies and initiatives would propel the company into—and even beyond—the better performers? What is required to sustain that level of performance? These are the kinds of insights executive buyers want from you. You don't have to have all the answers, but just tell them something they don't know.

You may be thinking this sounds like a lot of work, which it can be. But our sales clients tell us it's worth it. As we said earlier, it helps you better assess your customer's financial performance and potentially identify areas of opportunities. And don't forget a common theme in the interviews we conducted with executive buyers is they want you to TELL THEM SOMETHING THEY DON'T KNOW!

Profitability

Profitability is another key area of financial performance. It is often used as part of executive compensation. There are lots of different measures of profitability. We are using what is call Operating Income Margin. Operating Income is revenue less all operating costs such as Cost of Goods Sold; selling, general and administration; and depreciation and amortization. Operating Income Margin is Operating Income expressed as a percentage of revenue.

It is important to understand profitability at the industry level since it is an important driver for the ability to grow and maintain the business, innovate, and invest in your solutions. As you review industry profitability, think about your customers. What are the more profitable ones doing differently? How have your solutions helped them? What can you tell less profitable customers that they don't know?

Profitability, like revenue growth, varies by industry. Figure 2-7 shows profitability for a variety of industries headquartered in North America with $1 billion or more in annual revenue. Pharmaceuticals tend to have the highest Operating Income Margin. You may be thinking, *"So that's why drugs are so darn expensive!"* That's a discussion for another day. But an industry's profit margin is driven by several factors such as the value their products and services deliver, the risks associated with providing products and services, and the amount needed to invest in assets. The pharmaceutical industry provides lifesaving drugs which is of extremely high value and incurs substantial risks in bringing new drugs to market. It is estimated that it costs over $1 billion to bring a new drug to market. Some estimates top $2 billion. So it is not surprising at all that

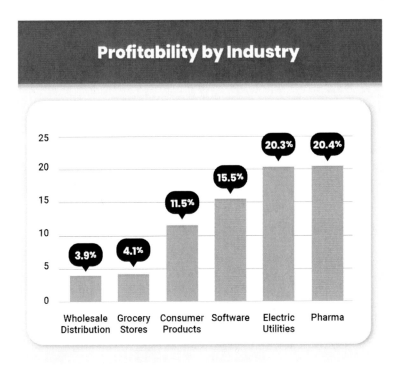

Figure 2-7. Five-year average profitability varies significantly by industry, shown here for the years 2015–2019. Source: FinListics ClientIQ.

it has one of the higher profit margins. By comparison, wholesale distribution has one of the lowest profit margins. Why? Wholesale distribution provides an important service. But not much value is added to the products that are provided and risks are lower.

We talked earlier about the influence of how much an industry needs to invest in assets to generate revenue and how this tends to influence profitability. Wholesale distribution, for example, on average invest $0.10 in fixed assets such as distribution centers per $1.00 in revenue. By comparison, an electric utility on average for $1.00 in revenue invests around $3.50 in assets such as generation, transmission, and distribution. As a result, wholesale distribution can earn a competitive return on a much lower profit margin. Whereas electric utilities need a much higher profit margin to earn a return attractive to investors given its heavy investments in assets.

Figure 2-8, "Industry Profitability: Consumer Products," shows the average and better performers for consumer products headquartered in North America with over $1 billion in revenue. A couple of observations:

- The better performers' profitability is a little over 40 percent higher than the average's, which is significant.

- Both the better performers' and the average's profitability are down from their peak years.

To better understand the difference between the better performers and the average, you'd look at factors such as product mix, pricing strategy, and better management of business trends, such as shifts in the retail operating model, and adoption of technologies such as digital technology shown in Figure 2-2. Again, the goal is to understand the industry so you can tell the buyer something they don't know.

You would also want to understand why profitability is off from its best years. For example, have materials, labor, and distribution costs increased? Have prices fallen? More regulation? Insight around these factors helps you better empathize with your customer and often provides areas to explore further with the customer. Let's say manufacturing labor

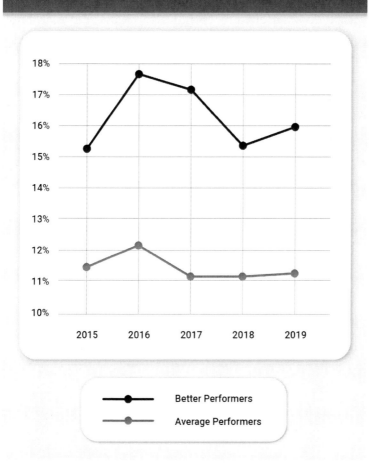

Figure 2-8. Profitability for consumer products companies headquartered in North America with over $1 billion in revenue, 2015–2019. Source: FinListics ClientIQ.

costs have risen and you sell automation equipment. You could use the increase in labor costs to show how your solution can help lower these costs and help increase profitability. We have seen companies use this kind of knowledge to work with individual customers and also to develop marketing campaigns that better show the business outcomes benefits of their solutions.

INSIGHT-LED SELLING IN ACTION

Action: Assess industry financial performance

Purpose: Understand the influence of industry forces on you customer's financial performance

1. Go to step 2 if you have access to data on your customer's industry financial performance. If not, go to www.InsightLedSelling.com and download financial data for an industry representative of your customer. Use the code INSIGHTSELLER to access the site.

2. Assess the performance of revenue growth or profitability and answer these questions. If you are energetic, assess both.

    a. For the average performers, is there a trend?

    b. What are some factors that are causing the trend?

c. What are some factors that could be causing
the gap between the average performers and
the better performers?

d. How have/could your solutions help the
average performers move closer to the better
performers?

Step 4: Understand Common Industry Goals and Strategies

In Chapter 1, "Executive Insights," we highlighted the importance of knowing your customer goals and strategies to better communicate with executives, and in Chapter 3, "Line of Business Insights," we will explore in more detail the importance of knowing customer-specific goals and strategies. Knowing goals and strategies common to specific industries is also beneficial for the following reasons:

- Helps you to create industry-specific solution playbooks that are scalable across many customers

- Provides a framework to compare your customer's specific goals with industry goals

- Is a useful conversation starter when engaging with private companies whose goals are often not publicly available

You probably thought we were going to also list knowing common industry goals helps build credibility and have better conversations with executives. You're right; it does. But you already guessed that.

Identifying common industry goals and strategies is a key responsibility of product marketing. There are many ways to identify common industry goals and strategies. For example:

- Research of individual customers

- Social media searches

- Customer surveys

We recommend conducting research of individual customers by industry, focusing on industry leaders. This helps to discover not only common industry goals and strategies but also the initiatives of individual lines of business. Augment this with social media searches. Customer surveys can be of value, though they typically have a low response rate.

Figure 2-9 provides examples of common goals and strategies for Consumer Products Industry based on FinListics' research of individual companies.

It shouldn't come as a surprise that companies within an industry often have similar goals. They deal with the same environmental factors. They also tend to hire the same consultants, who may provide the same guidance. Breakout organizations such as Amazon differentiate themselves as leaders, mastering the landscape and accomplishing industry goals a whole new way, leaving businesses like Macy's and Sears scrambling to catch up. Your customers may have

Examples of Common Goals and Strategies in Consumer Products Industry	
Goal	**Strategies Supporting Goal**
Drive Revenue Growth	• Build strong product portfolio • Enhance customer experience • Expand omnichannel reach • Enhance customer retention
Expand Profitability	• Improve efficiencies • Optimize operations • Maintain best-in-class talent • Implement sustainability initiatives
Mitigate Risk across the Enterprise	• Develop cyber resilience • Mitigate operational risk

Figure 2-9. Examples of Common Goals and Strategies in the Consumer Products Industry.

fallen far behind; your broader perspective and input can prove invaluable.

Get to know your customer's industry so you can address them with confidence, share your observations with executives, and build credibility, opening the door to more opportunities. You don't have to be an industry expert, but it's essential to have an informed point of view, which means doing your homework regarding the key issues we've highlighted in this chapter. Taking the time to do the legwork will set you apart from the competition in a big way.

INSIGHT-LED SELLING IN ACTION

Action: Identify common industry goals and strategies

Purpose: Start building industry playbook on how your solutions deliver business outcomes

To help with this action, go to www.InsightLedSelling.com for examples of common goals and strategies for select industries. Use the code INSIGHTSELLER to access the site.

1. What is a common goal for one of the industries you sell into?

2. What are a few common strategies supporting that goal?

3. Develop an elevator pitch in nontechnical terms about how your solutions help implement one of these strategies and achieve the goal.

STEP 5: IDENTIFY BUYERS' SUPPORTING GOALS AND STRATEGIES

Consider the benefits of knowing the buyer's supporting common industry goals and strategies:

- Better understand what matters most to your traditional buyers

- Identify potential new buyers

- Provide a baseline to which you can compare your individual customer's goals and strategies

The following are examples of potential buyers, by line of business, who align with the goal of driving growth:

- Product Development

- Sales and Marketing

- Information Technology

- Customer Service

- Distribution and Logistics

Once you have identified the buyers for your customer's industry, answer the following questions:

- Which buyers do you currently target?

- Are there some additional buyers you would want to talk to? The answer to this question is most often yes!

STEP 6: IDENTIFY BUYERS' INITIATIVES AND OPERATIONAL KPIS

Knowing the buyer's initiatives and Operational KPIs offers powerful benefits:

- Provides a framework for you to tell the story about how your solutions deliver business outcomes and by how much

- Helps you tailor your business outcomes message for individual buyers

- Identifies new areas of opportunity with existing and often new buyers

And of course, as with all of the steps, knowing the initiatives and Operational KPIs also builds confidence and credibility.

Figure 2-10 provides examples of initiatives and Operational KPIs for some of the Consumer Products buyers in the above steps 4 and 5. Supporting the goal drives revenue growth. This is not a comprehensive list but offered simply for illustrative purposes. Some of the Operational KPIs are common across the different lines of business while others are unique. Common KPIs include the following:

- Net Promoter Score

- Customer retention

- Cross-sell/upsell

- New customer revenue

It is not likely that your solutions provide benefits to all buyers. Start with those that are the most relevant and dig deeper into their initiatives. Our experience is that sellers often don't know why buyers are really buying. They are really buying to implement their initiatives in support of the strategies and goals. It is also recommended that you also explore some other buyers' initiatives and Operational KPIs. We have heard that doing so helped identify new opportunities.

Use the initiatives and Operational KPIs to tell a story with a business outcomes focus. Not a technology focus. Let's say your company sells product development process software. Marketing is creating collateral targeting VPs of Product Development. The message, for example, could talk about how companies are using your solution to better generate ideas, product roadmaps, and product marketing. And how this helps them launch new products that are viewed as more valuable by consumers and more effectively compete with private label brand. This increases the number of new products launched annually with a higher success rate, which helps drives higher revenue. Ideally, the collateral would also include insights into how much improvement was delivered.

Within the context of your customer's situation, describe

Examples of Lines of Businesses' Initiatives and Operational KPIs Supporting Goal of Driving Revenue in Consumer Products		
Line of Business	**Initiatives**	**Unique Line of Business Operational KPIs**
Product Development	• Collaborate with customers on improved products to discover new niche markets and extend life cycles • Faster R&D, speed to market, and launch timelines for new products	• Time to market • Product success rate • Number of new products launched
Customer Service	• Offer self-service chat bot technology and virtual agent tools to personalize and speed up customer service • Improve seamless returns process	• First response time • First-time resolution • Time to resolution
Distribution and Logistics	• Respond to consumer demand for fast shipping • Manage reverse logistics and maximize value of returned inventory	• Customer order cycle time • On-time deliveries • Order accuracy

Figure 2-10. Examples of Lines of Business Supporting Goal of Driving Revenue Growth in Consumer Products and Their Initiatives and Operational KPIs.

what your solution offers. What's your value proposition within the industry in terms of growing revenue, increasing profits, or better managing assets? How do you propose achieving these goals? Then discuss how you measure the impact of your solution. The customer won't realize its full value overnight, so you need to outline the timeline and hurdles to realizing that value after they make the purchase. Make a specific case for Return on Investment, aligning the industry, the company, and the solution.

Identifying and analyzing an industry's key elements takes time and effort, and you'll make faster progress if you make it a team sport. Do your own research, but reach out to sales colleagues, solution architects, industry experts, and product development too. Ask them how your solution addresses the industry's core elements and your customer's situation.

Ultimately, create a playbook for each industry. You may have to do this on your own, but if your sales and marketing support teams have the bandwidth, try to offload the documentation and some of the research. This way, you won't have to reinvent the wheel every time you get in front of a new customer. Ideally, these playbooks become living documents with regular contributions from within the company and the field and oversight from a knowledge management team.

STEP 7: CREATE AN INDUSTRY PLAYBOOK

An industry playbook aligns your solutions to the information in the previous steps 1–6 and shown in Figure 2-1, "Knowing Your Customer's Industry Key Elements," and offers the following benefits:

- Builds organizational alignment on your solutions' business outcomes

- Helps scale sales

- Motivates deeper exploration into your solutions' business outcomes

Remember, building an industry playbook is a team sport requiring participation from product development, sales and marketing, solution architects, industry experts, and so forth. Also, common themes in creating an industry playbook are:

- How in nontechnical terms your solutions deliver business outcomes

- How much financial benefits are delivered

- Telling buyers something they don't know

The following is a recommended outline using the steps we have explored in the chapter.

Step 1: Industry Business Technology Trends

- Which ones represent the biggest opportunities/threats to your customers?

- How can your solutions help customers leverage these trends?

- What are some things you can tell buyers they don't know about managing these trends?

Step 2: Industry Risk Factors

- Which are the highest sources of risk in the near and long term?

- How are the better companies managing these risks?

- How do your solutions help?

Step 3: Industry Financial Performance

- What are the two to three Areas of Financial Performance your solutions help customers better manage? Why?

- What are factors causing trends over time and differences in the average and better performers?

- Which of these factors do your solutions help better manage?

Step 4: Common Industry Goals and Strategies

- What industry goals do your solutions help customers achieve?

- For these goals, what strategies do your solutions help customers implement?

- What can you tell buyers something they may not know about the goals and strategies your solutions can help?

Step 5: Buyers Supporting Goals and Strategies

- Who are the key buyers supporting the goals and strategies that would find you solutions of value?

- Are there potentially any new buyers?

- What is your plan for reaching out to new buyers?

Step 6: Buyers' Initiatives and Operational KPIs

- For each buyer identified in step 5, what are the initiatives and Operational KPIs supported by your solutions?

- Case Studies

  * How do your solutions help implement these initiatives?

  * By how much do your solutions improve the Operational KPIs and what is the financial benefit?

- What can you tell the buyers about their initiatives they may not know?

SUMMARY

Insight around your customer's industry takes time, but by simply being aware of the fact that industries have unique goals, strategies, initiatives, Operational and financial KPIs, trends, risks, and opportunities will make you more sensitive to this information when it's presented. You may be astonished by how much information is available once you've made the conscious decision to tune into the essentials and learn the language around them.

Following the seven steps gives you a framework for methodically learning your customer's industry, and as you build a playbook, you'll begin to see how all the pieces fit together. This will give you a perspective closer to that of the executive buyer, which is exactly what you want: to be able to see their business and their challenges from their point of view. This will also give you a whole new perspective on your solution so you can talk about it in a way that actually matters to customers.

As you build your industry knowledge, you will also see that the unique goals, strategies, initiatives, Operational and financial KPIs, trends, risks, and opportunities that exist between industries are further divided by line of business. Fortunately, your commitment to Insight-Led Selling has provided a foundation with executive insights and industry insights on which to further build your customer knowledge at a deeper and more granular level: line of business insights.

INDUSTRY INSIGHTS BEST PRACTICES

Increase your rate of success by expanding your industry knowledge. Insight-Led Selling's best practices will help you become a more knowledgeable seller that gets noticed—instead of overlooked—by executive buyers.

- Competitors within an industry share common circumstances and key drivers of success, risks, opportunities, and trends, so knowing what's happening in the industry tells you something about what's happening with your customer. Know the industry and you will know your buyer.

- Know your customer's industry's key terms and use them in your conversations with executive buyers.

- Get to the point and be specific. Address a single business driver or KPI and be prepared to explain how, where, and why you can solve a problem and provide strong results. Offer powerful observations, insights, and ideas, and link your solution to the Operational and financial KPIs and business outcomes.

LINE OF BUSINESS INSIGHTS

"Let me tell you about a couple of examples of a best and a worst sales call.

"When we were looking at automated sourcing solutions, we set up one-hour calls with two vendors, a day apart. The first vendor had clearly done their homework. They spent the first seventeen minutes of the call verifying what they knew and getting clarification on what they didn't, asking a lot of questions about our business and the problem we were trying to solve. Only then did they shift to 'Let us show you our solution.' They explained how it could work for us, and after some discussion we were confident enough to say, 'We like what we're seeing. What's the next step?'

"Per our typical due diligence, we still wanted to talk to the other vendor and see how they compared. Well, they didn't. On that call, the seller immediately went into demo mode: speeds and feeds and how their solution would take care of all our needs. Instead of asking questions, they made

assumptions about our back-office technology. If they had been curious enough to ask, they would have discovered their assumptions were wrong and they were taking us in the wrong direction. That call ended twenty-eight minutes early. It was the last time we talked to them."

—JUSTIN HONAMAN, former VP/GM, Analytics, Data & Digital Transformation, Strategic Sourcing & Procurement, Georgia Pacific

Establishing your credibility and earning trust on the road from vendor to trusted advisor—and eventually, strategic partner—requires knowing your customer's industry, as discussed in the previous chapter. You also need to tailor the message of your solution's business and financial benefits to a growing number of stakeholders who want you to address their individual needs, issues, and interests.

A study by Gartner estimates that in large B2B deals, there are more than ten stakeholders.[5] That's ten or more stakeholders all trying to accomplish something and looking to you for a single solution. And even though they're all ultimately working toward the same company goal, each one measures success differently.

Your solution needs to align with the company's overarching goals and strategies *and* each stakeholder's initiatives and metrics, and the more specifically you can address them, the better. The head of manufacturing, for example, won't be very impressed to hear that you can help reduce costs at the company level. Instead, they'd like to hear about how your

---

5   Spencer Wixom, "84 Percent of Customers Report a Buying Journey Taking Longer than Expected," Challenger.com, November 21, 2018, https://www.challengerinc.com/blog/more-b2b-decision-makers-want-in/.

solution improves manufacturing costs per unit, say, through increased capital utilization and lower unplanned downtime. Likewise, marketing is less interested in a generic statement about how your solution will help increase revenue than it is in learning how your solution helps improve customer insights resulting in more personalized offers, which will drive higher revenue through reduced customer churn and increased cross-sell/upsell.

Generally speaking, simply saying your solution can help reduce costs or increase revenue isn't only vague—it's boring. And they're probably hearing the same thing from every other salesperson. To get a decision maker's attention, describe your offerings in the context of their individual initiatives and how they get measured, their "scorecard."

Line of business insights benefit you for many reasons including the following:

- Helps you identify potential stakeholders in the company that you may not have considered

- Allows you to tailor your message for these individual buyers accordingly

- Deepens your enterprise relationship with the customer

Insight-Led Selling provides the framework for sellers to better understand the alignment between each line of business stakeholder's initiatives supporting company-wide goals and strategies, and their measures of success, which we call Operational Key Performance Indicators (KPIs), and how to communicate the business and financial benefits of your solutions to each business unit more effectively.

Figure 3-1 illustrates the results of a survey that we and one of our partners, Revegy, provided to sales teams on how well they tailor their message for individual line of business buyers. Just over one-quarter of the respondents believe they're doing a good job. Although this could be viewed as disappointing, the good news is that salespeople and their management are aware of their shortcoming, and many are striving to make progress—no doubt due to their realization that there is extreme value in this skill.

Relying on being comfortable with speaking to only one line of business is a sure way to set yourself up for failure, especially on large deals or with strategic accounts. Many other units potentially have veto power. You have to get out of your comfort zone, identify all the decision makers, and learn how to approach them. Basically, you have to answer the question, "Who are these people, and how do I talk to them?"

In addition to knowing your solution's features and function, it's even more important to know what your customer wants from those solutions. As an example, a banking customer was looking to get some new analytics to help with auto loan underwriting. The chief risk officer (CRO) had this notion around a unique risk profile that the bank could put around loans for a particular auto make and model that borrowers typically paid off quickly. For those loans, the bank might want to increase the credit score risk and charge a little more interest, allowing the CRO to further grow the business.

His team had figured out, through analytics, which prospects were most likely to pay off the loans despite their lower credit scores. The bank could extend credit to those borrow-

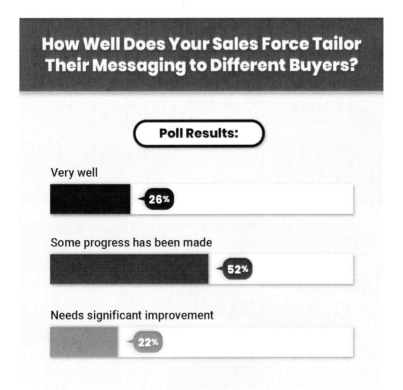

Figure 3-1. Although many sales teams believe they are making progress, there remains a lot of opportunity for improvement around tailoring messaging to different buyers.

ers at a higher interest rate and increase the consumer lending portfolio. To accomplish his goal, the CRO needed a report that showed live data modeling and data visualization.

The seller showed up with a dashboard and lots of reports and spent several minutes stepping the executive through all the bells and whistles. They were so used to doing the "tech talk" with technology buyers that they didn't know how to speak the CRO's language. This was a different buyer in a different line of business who didn't have the time or the patience for a dog-and-pony show, and his reaction was blunt and to the point: "Why the hell do I care about these pretty reports or what they look like? I'm trying to solve a problem around consumer lending. Give me that solution."

Fancy dashboards and reports don't matter to an executive who needs a solution that can take a deep dive into analytics and choose good lending prospects.

When you pitch a solution, it's important to know *why* you're doing so and how it can help advance the customer's top priorities in a concrete way. Skip the parts that don't matter and get straight to the solution. A CRO doesn't specialize in dashboards—they specialize in driving revenue and mitigating risk. Give them what they need to do their job.

IT TAKES A VILLAGE

"Know your audience. If you're meeting with five people from five lines of business, don't walk in thinking you can talk about just finance or just marketing. Be prepared to talk about whatever each one of those people cares about, because it's going to be different for every one of them."

—CFO OF a community bank

Gartner's findings and the results of our own poll provide the backdrop for an example project that has multiple stakeholders or lines of business and illustrates the importance of tailoring your message.

Say you have a retail client whose goal is to grow revenue by implementing a strategy of expanding the use of their omni-channel. The customer has both a website and physical stores. Suppose your solution provides greater customer insight and helps unify the customer experience from purchase to delivery. As we review the example, try to answer these questions:

- Which lines of business are responsible for rollout?

- How would your conversation need to be tailored to talk to the different business units?

Figure 3-2 shows some of the stakeholders involved in this project and examples of their individual initiatives. Some of their measures of success are shown below. Although not complete, these initiatives and their associated measures of success highlight the need to tailor your message to the different lines of business.

- Marketing wants greater customer insights to better understand demand and to create personalized offerings.

   * Campaign response rates and customer retention

- Merchandising wants to better understand current and future changes in demand and to ensure product consistency across all sales channels.

   * Sell-through rates and percentage markdowns

- Customer care is focused on ensuring a consistent customer experience across all channels.

* Net Promoter Score (NPS); lifetime value of customer

- Distribution and Logistics will need to reconfigure the network to have shorter delivery times.

  * Customer order cycle time and Orders Delivered On Time

- Store operations must allow for Buy Online and Pick Up in Store (BOPIS) and Buy Online and Return in Store (BORIS).

  * Customer wait time and store labor costs

- Information Technology will work to create a mobile experience that provides a great user experience.

  * Number of downloads and uptime

- Human Resources will provide training for lines of business such as Distribution and Logistics and stores whose operations will be significantly impacted.

  * Employee satisfaction and turnover

- Finance will need to be convinced all of this is a solid idea and provide funding.

  * Return on Investment and Payback

Experience shows that one of the greatest benefits of creating a "village" of stakeholders around your customer's key projects is that it helps identify new buyers.

INSIGHT-LED SELLING IN ACTION

Action: Build an executive buyers' village

Purpose: Identify multiple stakeholders that influence your opportunity

You can download the FinListics "It Takes a Village" template from www.InsightLedSelling.com to help complete this action. Use the code INSIGHTSELLER to access the site. Ideally, you will complete this action using customer-specific data, but you can also complete it using common industry goals, strategies, and initiatives available on our website for select industries.

1. For one of your customers, select a goal and a strategy supporting that goal for which your solutions can help deliver a desired business outcome. For example, increase revenue (goal) by enhancing omnichannel experience (strategy), or expand profitability (goal) by improving operational efficiencies (strategy).

2. Identify some lines of business that are supporting this goal and strategy.

3. For the lines of business in step 2, identify one initiative supporting the strategy and goal.

4. For which of these lines of business can your solutions deliver business outcomes?

5. Did this action help you identify new lines of business to talk to?

FIVE INSIGHTS FOR SELLING INTO LINES OF BUSINESS

"When you're selling a project to multiple stakeholders, don't just run to whomever you think has the money. Your sales leadership may be pushing you to follow the money and get close to the CFO or CIO, but if the business decision maker is the CMO, you can't just go around them to get the deal done. That's how you burn relationships. Take each stakeholder into account. Sometimes it's a careful dance. As a technology seller, sales leadership will press for progress on the account—proposing, pitching, and escalating—and the caution here is that pushed too far, the customer could decide to find a different, more collaborative, business-focused, non-salesy partner."

—JUSTIN HONAMAN, former VP/GM, Analytics, Data & Digital Transformation, Strategic Sourcing & Procurement, Georgia Pacific

Figure 3-2. Especially for large deals, it takes a village of stakeholders and lines of business to move a deal to the finish line.

In Chapter 2, we talked about gaining insight into your customers' industries and creating a playbook for documenting what you learn about each one. You can leverage that knowledge within individual lines of business.

Insight-Led Selling proposes five insights, basically "things you need to know" to have meaningful conversations and successful engagements with buying executives within the various lines of business in your deals:

1. Company-wide goals

2. Strategies for achieving company-wide goals

3. Line of business aligned with goals and strategies

4. Lines of business's initiatives supporting goals and strategies

5. Lines of business's financial and Operational KPIs related to initiatives

As you collect this information about your customer, ask yourself these questions:

- How do my solutions help?

- What have I learned that I can provide to my executive buyer as additional insights into their situation, issues, and potential solutions beyond what they already know?

- Are there other buyers I could be selling to?

Now let's dive into the five insights for selling into lines of business.

Insight #1: Company-wide Goals

Companies set goals as a means to keep moving forward and focus people's attention on what matters the most. It is vitally important that what you are proposing is aligned with at least one of your customer's goals. Know all of your customer's goals and uncover areas of opportunity that you may not have thought about. Focus on those goals where your solution can have the greatest impact. Otherwise, what you are proposing will be of little or no value to executive buyers. Remember, they are often bonused on achieving these goals.

You often hear the term "SMART Goals":

- S = Specific

- M = Measurable

- A = Achievable

- R = Relevant

- T = Time-bound

Let's apply SMART to a real-world company, a global Consumer Packaged Goods (CPG) company with over $15 billion in revenue.

Specific

Reduce annual selling, general and administrative expense (SG&A), manufacturing operating costs, and logistics costs

Measurable

Realize over $600 million in annual savings

Achievable

Company has had successful cost reduction programs in the past, so there is a level of confidence that it can be done again. On a side note, company leaders have made this commitment to investors, so they better deliver!

Relevant

Profitability has trended down over the last five years. Need to improve profitability to fund higher revenue growth and provide greater returns to shareholders.

Time-bound

Saving will be achieved within two years and sustainable thereafter.

Sources of Goals: The annual report is often a good place to find a company's goals and strategies. The top executives of a company write a "letter to Shareholders" that provides an overview of the company's position, achievements related to past goals, and what they are focused on for the future. Additionally, in regulatory filings such as a Form 10K for companies domiciled in the United States or 20-F for companies not domiciled in the United States but traded in the United States, the Business Overview in this report may define goals and strategies as well. All publicly traded companies regardless of where they are domiciled and traded are required to file annual and what we call interim reports (quarterly or semi-annually) with regulatory authorities. For even more details about a company's goals, investor presentations and earnings call transcripts are a good source as well.

Barriers to Identifying Company-wide Goals

Sellers are typically very comfortable calling on the "friendly" people in the account. These people may be able to make *tactical* buying decisions, but they may lack the position and authority to make *strategic* decisions. If your buyer is the recipient of the budget rather than the creator of the budget, they may not have the leverage required to approve a deal. You need to be speaking with the budget creators and discovering their goals.

Note that even if you do identify the company-wide goals, your buyer may not have thought through the process of how to achieve them. This is where you can help, but it's also where another common barrier appears: sellers worry that understanding the goals of each individual stakeholder—as opposed to simply mastering the details of their product—takes time. It can take time, but it is well worth the effort since executive buyers expect you to know their goals, especially since those goals are in the public domain.

Too often, sellers don't know the answers to core questions around their customer's goals. When asked, they might say, "I think they're trying to move their business to the cloud." In the first place, that may be a project, but it's not a goal. They need to know the actual goal and how this initiative will help them achieve that goal. Salespeople aren't lazy; they want to do a good job and make sales. The problem is that they just don't know what they don't know—or *should* know—and when they do, they don't know how to get the information. Insight-Led Selling provides a method for developing your skills in their area.

Insight #2: Strategies

A company's strategy is a general direction the company sets for itself and its various elements to achieve a desired goal. In our example, the CPG company's strategies to achieve the $600 million+ cost savings comprise the following:

- Expanding Commercial Hubs

    * Cluster single-country subsidiaries into more efficient regional hubs

- Extending Shared Business Services and Streamlining Global Functions

    * Centralize finance and accounting and other functions

- Optimizing Global Supply Chain and Facilities

    * Consolidate production and Distribution and Logistics

Sources of Strategies: Good sources of strategies are annual reports, investor presentations, and earnings calls.

Once you know the business units' strategies, think about how your solutions can help implement those strategies and where you have helped other companies implement similar strategies. Suppose you offer Business Processing Outsourcing (BPO) services. You would focus on the strategy of *"extending shared business services and streamlining global units and more specifically, centralizing finance and accounting and other functions."* You would want to know the cost-savings goal for centralizing these functions. You would need to answer some questions too: Does the customer want to keep these services internal? Is the customer's intention to outsource these services or consider outsourcing these services? Where are your BPO services being applied that would be of interest to the customer? It is still very early in the sales process, but what would the business outcomes cost savings be if you could deliver to the customer the same level of benefits your solutions have delivered to other customers?

A seller that can match their solution to a strategy, and that strategy to a goal, connects the dots, so to speak, for the buyer. For example, a network provider we worked with was talking to a hotel chain about wireless services. The sellers were well into their pitch when they paused to ask, "What are you going to do with this wireless service?" It turned out the hotel was working on an automatic check-in mobile room access app (initiative) to improve customer experience (strategy) that would increase revenue (goal). The sales team pivoted to explain how they could help deliver that outcome, and they ended up landing the multi-hundred-million-dollar deal. Doing so, though, required going beyond talking about their wireless products and specifically addressing how those products would support the customer's intended end use.

Insight #3: Lines of Business Aligned with Goals and Strategies

"Corporate strategy is a great starting point for sellers, and I'm fine with them asking me about how my individual goals align with that strategy. Think about it: Do you want a seller talking to you from a place of complete ignorance about your goals, or one who has a high-level understanding of your company's strategies and takes the initiative to ask questions, gather information, and gain an understanding of what you're trying to accomplish?"

—TOM SCHMITT, Chairman, President, and CEO, Forward Air Corp.

Now it's time to identify how those lines of business align with goals and strategies. An approach we like is to first think about the Areas of Financial Performance that are the focus of the goals and strategies. Let's focus on the strategy "Optimizing Global Supply Chain and Facilities." This would drive the goal to reduce the Cost of Goods Sold. It would also increase the utilization of manufacturing and distribution assets and possibly lower the investment in inventory. Therefore, the Areas of Financial Performance improved by this strategy include the following:

- Cost of Goods Sold as a percentage of revenue

- Fixed Asset Utilization

- Days in Inventory

The next step is to identify the relevant lines of business, which for this strategy comprise these units:

- Manufacturing

- Distribution and Logistics

Both would have operating costs impacted, as well as changes in facilities.

Other lines of business likely include the following:

- Human Resources, since reduction and relocation of personnel will be required

- IT, since optimization of production and distribution across facilities will be required

Sources of Lines of Business Aligned with Goals and Strategies: In Chapter 4, we will explore the Areas of Financial Performance by business unit. This is a good starting point for your research. Also, review investor presentations and earnings calls where sometimes line of business executives talk about the goals and strategies they are supporting.

Lack of awareness of a stakeholder's goals and strategies is more common than you can imagine, but the problem can be avoided with the right approach: thinking outside-in, talking to the right people, and getting real about your relationships with the buyer.

THINK OUTSIDE-IN

"My best single piece of advice to sellers is this: When targeting me or any other executive, make it very personal. I get emails that are obviously the result of blind targeting. Sellers can get to know me by reading blogs, articles, and interviews. They can get to know our business and what we're trying to accomplish. Know our brand. Shop our stores. Then send me an email that speaks to me, not everybody else."

—JO ANN HEROLD, Chief Marketing Officer,
The Honey Baked Ham Company

Sales problems tend to stem from a core mistake: sellers focus on themselves instead of the customer, meaning they come in with a product and push it, regardless of the customer's actual needs and goals. This phenomenon is known as the "inside-out" approach, as opposed to the "outside-in" approach. Customers know when you're just trying to sell them something—anything—to meet your quota.

We're not picking on sellers—we know about inside-out selling because we work with companies that do it all the time. We were working with a large logistics provider that was pitching to a major automotive company. A lot of the presentation wasn't about the customer but about the logistics company: how big it was, how it was operating in so many countries, and how it was extremely dependable and efficient. Not much was said about the automotive company's goals and the challenges they were facing. On the sales teams' way out, one of the automotive executives said, "Guess what? You guys are DUMB. You *Don't Understand My Business." Whoops.*

TALKING TO THE RIGHT PERSON

In another instance, we were working with a team that had come up with a clever way to save a potential buyer $5 million in IT costs. They wanted help on how to talk to the CFO, and we said, "We can, but that will be a waste of time." They were shocked, but we asked if they knew what the CFO actually *wanted*. An investor presentation indicated the business wanted to expand its profit margin. Achieving this would generate an additional $500 million in profits. We said, "So *someone* in the company is interested in $5 million, but it's not the CFO." The bad news was, they did not understand the customer's big-picture goals. The good news was, they found the right buyer for the $5 million saving and were inspired to look for other ways to help the customer expand margins that would be of interest to the CFO and other executives.

Another problem stems from sellers not talking to the person who has the ultimate decision-making power. They haven't done the research to know who has veto power and financial responsibility for the investment. So they call in to their traditional buying center and talk to the mid-level manager who has influence *but not the final say*. Maybe the seller feels afraid to have discussions with higher-level executives, or maybe they think this manager has a special relationship with someone in the C-suite. That special relationship might just mean the manager had coffee with the CIO once. The seller is not actually talking to the right person.

It's important to ask at the outset who is involved in making a purchasing decision. Do a little probing to find out who else needs to be sold on the product, directly or indirectly, and uncover any blind spots. If IT is responsible for implementing a digital marketing technology, those stakeholders will be the buyers, but they're not the end users. Marketing is the end user, so sometimes IT will bring marketing in, but sometimes it won't. The organization may silo those functions. If you're not talking to the end user, you need to provide the case they can pass along to that end user.

GETTING REAL ABOUT RELATIONSHIPS

"When you're selling a complex solution, you have to address the gauntlet of stakeholders. You need to know each person's desired business outcomes, but companies don't want sellers running all over the place and trying to figure out who to talk to, so you need a champion. If you have a relationship in IT, have a frank conversation with that person about how your solution addresses their business outcomes. Get them on your side, then ask for introductions to other stakeholders. And you better be credible. No one wants to use up relationship capital on a salesperson that can't effectively talk to other stakeholders—or worse, not deliver the goods."

—**JIM AUGUST,** VP of Enterprise Architecture
at a Fortune 500 Life Insurance Company

As you examine who the real decision makers are and what they need, it's time to get real about which buyers you have a strong relationship with and who you don't. Just because you've been in an elevator with someone once or had a few phone calls doesn't mean you know them or that they're prepared to discuss their goals and strategies with you. We've seen sellers overestimate their connection with an executive and walk out of a meeting believing they've made great headway, when in reality, that executive pointed them to a direct report. You can't assume you've been given a clear path forward; nine times out of ten, that action says you've been deferred.

If the executive says something like, "What you're offering is not immediately valuable to me, but it's probably valuable to someone who works for me," they are politely telling you, "I'm not interested; go bother someone else." You may have made it to the right decision maker, but they may already be running the initiative you're proposing to address, or maybe your solution isn't material enough for their needs. Without the right awareness and framework to address what matters to them, you could misinterpret the conversation and worse, blow the opportunity.

All of this is to say, yes, shame on the unprepared, but if you avoid these pitfalls and apply your research, you *will* reap the rewards. If you put in the time to find something tangible that will help the customer's business, whether from a financial perspective, or through increased agility, or with better risk management, then you will benefit too. You sell more and you'll faster.

Insight #4: Lines of Business's Initiatives Supporting Goals and Strategies

Initiatives are actions taken by a line of business with the purpose of implementing strategies and achieving the goals they support. Let's focus on the business units Manufacturing and Distribution and Logistics. Some of the initiatives related to the strategy "Optimizing Global Supply Chain and Facilities" *might including the following:*

- Manufacturing:

    * Leverage Internet of Things (IoT) to increase Capacity Utilization and lower unplanned downtime

    * Optimize production across all facilities

- Distribution and Logistics:

    * Improve collaboration with customers and suppliers

    * Improve inventory visibility

Learning even the most common line of business initiatives may seem like a lot of work and initially it can be. But like most activities, the more you perform it, the easier it becomes. It will also build your credibility with executive buyers. You can discuss their initiatives and compare them to other companies in their industry. Other good news is that companies in the same industry tend to have similar goals, strategies, and initiatives. Your research can be scalable across companies. It can also give you the opportunity to tell buyers something they don't know by comparing and contrasting your customer's initiatives to others in the industry.

Once you know the initiatives, focus on those that your

solutions can help implement. Suppose you offer products and services that can help with the manufacturing initiative *"leverage IoT to increase Capacity Utilization and lower unplanned downtime."* You would want to explore questions such as, "How much of the $600 million cost-savings goal is expected to come from manufacturing?" and "If your solutions could deliver business outcomes like they have for others in the industry, how much would be the contribution to manufacturing's cost-savings goals?" and "What might you be able to tell the buyer about implementing this initiative they may not know based on experiences with other customers in the industry?"

Sources of Lines of Business's Initiatives Supporting Goals and Strategies: To gain more insight into the different business units' initiatives, companies sometimes have each executive define initiatives and business outcomes relevant to their departments in investor presentations. These executives are also called on to discuss their areas during an earnings call meeting, which are usually presented in the earnings call transcript.

Insight #5: Lines of Business's Financial and Operational Key Performance Indicators (KPIs) Related to Initiatives

We know different players are involved in the decision making and that their focus areas and measures of success differ. So how do different buyers measure success? Each is focused on one or more Areas of Financial Performance and has their own KPIs by line of business. The business units' financial and Operational KPIs are some of the most important pieces of information you can have as a seller. These are on executives' dashboards; they are how they measure performance and success. Ultimately, your solutions can improve some of these KPIs. That's why it's crucial that you be able to articulate *how your solutions improve these KPIs and by how much.*

AREAS OF FINANCIAL PERFORMANCE AND OPERATIONAL KEY PERFORMANCE INDICATORS (KPIS)

AREAS OF FINANCIAL PERFORMANCE ARE items such as how fast a company is growing revenue, which is called revenue growth; managing profitability, which is revenue less operating expenses expressed as a percentage of revenue; and asset utilization, which is how many dollars of revenue are generated for a dollar invested in assets such as inventory and production assets. These measures of performance all come from a company's financial statements. The Areas of Financial Performance are used by executives to manage the business and measure performance. Investors use the Areas of Financial Performance to assess how well the business is being managed, and to make decisions such as whether to invest more or less in a company.

Operational Key Performance Indicators (KPIs), as the name implies, measures performance at an operational level. Areas of Financial Performance are a manifestation of how well a company is managing the activities underlying the Operational KPIs. Everyone reading this book can identify with the area of financial performance revenue growth. Operational KPIs associated with revenue growth include customer retention, cross-sell/upsell, new customers, and closure rate. The higher these KPIs, the higher the revenue growth. It's imperative you know which Operational KPIs are improved by your solutions because ultimately, that is how you help customers improve financial performance.

Sources of Financial and Operational KPIs: Financial KPIs are found on the income statement and balance sheet. Again, you don't have to be an expert, but here are some considerations to get you started. For the strategy we are exploring for both Manufacturing and Distribution and Logistics, the financial KPIs are those that we identified earlier:

- Cost of Goods Sold

- Fixed Asset Utilization

- Days in Inventory

Operational KPIs are quantifiable metrics used to plan, evaluate, and improve business performance. They are what really drives the financial KPIs. For example, for Manufacturing, Operational KPIs typically include the following:

- Materials, labor, and overhead costs per unit

- Capacity Utilization

- Unplanned Machine Downtime

For Distribution and Logistics, Operational KPIs typically include the following:

- Transportation and Warehousing Costs as Percent of Revenue

- Order Fill Rate

- Orders Delivered On Time

Figure 3-3 provides examples of Operational KPIs for a sample of lines of business. A more complete set of business units is available at InsightLedSelling.com, code INSIGHTSELLER.

Being aware of each unit's KPIs can lead you to new entry points into the business. For example, a computer software salesperson was calling on a drugstore. He planned to speak with the technology team. But then he thought about what the software was actually *enabling*. It wasn't going to solve IT's problems. They would make the buy, install it, and support it. But his solution wouldn't necessarily make their lives easier or help them meet their goals.

The sales guy knew the software could improve the company's *supply chain*. So he dug around and found the name of the person in charge. With no appointment scheduled, he fortu-

How Is Success Measured?

Marketing

- Number of campaigns
- Response rate
- Price optimization
- Cross-sell/upsell
- New customers

Information Technology

- Application development expense
- Application management expense
- IT spend per employee
- Return on IT investment
- Projects delivered on time/on budget

Customer Care

- Net Promoter Score
- Customer retention
- First-time resolution
- Customer satisfaction by channel
  (web chat, IVR, service rep, etc.)

Human Resources

- Employee satisfaction
- Employee turnover
- Cost of recruiting, development, and retention

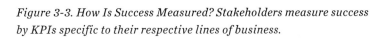

Figure 3-3. How Is Success Measured? Stakeholders measure success by KPIs specific to their respective lines of business.

itously ran into the supply chain manager and spoke about "Days in Inventory," knowing his software could improve that metric. The manager's ears immediately perked up. "Come with me," he said. "I'm in the middle of something, but we need to talk." The salesperson drove the man to the airport—the guy was literally on his way to get on a plane—and they talked the whole way.

He had never used the phrase "Days in Inventory" and hadn't expected that response. The supply chain manager had always seen the sales guy as a technology vendor, selling solutions that didn't concern him. With one phrase, mentioning one metric that mattered to the buyer, the salesperson changed the whole conversation.

TYING IT ALL TOGETHER

Figure 3-4 provides a framework for tying together the five insights for selling into lines of business. It is useful for both account planning and engaging with executive buyers. We use the CPG company's goal of finding $600 million in cost and the related strategy of "Optimizing Global Supply Chain and Facilities," and the two lines of business Manufacturing and Distribution and Logistics. Buyer alignment framework examples for the banking and insurance industries are included in the Chapter 3 section of the appendix.

This is a collaborative effort, where you can make some assumptions and take them to the customer to help narrow down their focus and draw out the details. It shows that you've done your homework and gives them and you a framework around their individual goals and strategies that they had not

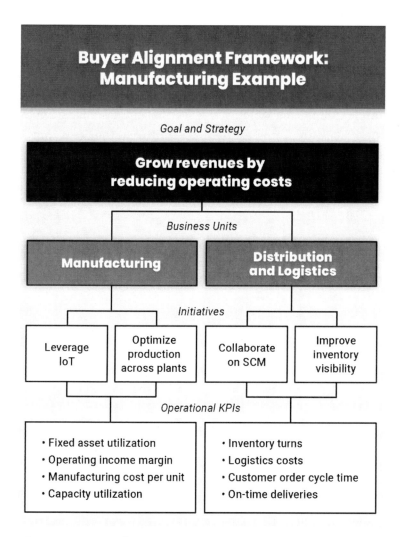

Figure 3-4. Buyer Alignment Framework for tying together your insights on customer's goals, strategies, and supporting lines of business initiatives and Operational KPIs.

previously shared with you. Consider this framework customer ready. First, use it to organize your thoughts, research, and assumptions about who's responsible for what. Then take it to the customer to review and validate. It leads to a collaborative discussion during which you'll see that the customer will be more likely to share information about what they're trying to do and how they're trying to do it.

INSIGHT-LED SELLING IN ACTION

Action: Create a buyers alignment framework

Purpose: Begin to tailor the message for stakeholders that will address their point of value

You can build on your responses to the Build an Executive Buyers Village action to help complete this action. Buyer Alignment Framework examples for the banking and the insurance industries appear in the Chapter 3 section of the appendix of this book.

You can also download the FinListics "Buyers Alignment Framework" template from www.InsightLedSelling.com to help complete this action. Use the code INSIGHTSELLER to access the site.

Ideally, you would complete this action using customer-specific information. But to get started, our website provides examples of common industry goals and strategies for select industries and for lines of business, their initiatives, financial metrics, and Operational KPIs.

1. For one of your customers, select a goal and a strategy supporting that goal for which your solutions can help deliver a desired business outcome.

2. Select two lines of business (LOBs) supporting the goal and strategy that your solutions can help.

3. For each LOB, identify two initiatives. For these initiatives, select some Areas of Financial Performance and Operational KPIs that the LOBs will use to measure success.

4. Complete the Buyers Alignment Framework. See Figure 3-4 as an example.

5. How will you use the Buyers Alignment Framework in account planning?

6. How will you use the framework with customers?

SUMMARY

The many stakeholders within each line of business and in every industry that make up your customer base are all people—just like you, just like us. They don't expect you to know everything. They know you will never understand their industry and business as well as they do, but even making an attempt goes a long way. You're not going to get it 100 percent right—that's impossible. But neglecting to make the effort is like going to a different country and just speaking English the whole time versus at least learning and using some basic, polite phrases. Even if your accent is terrible, you see the difference in locals' faces. They respond much more favorably to the person who tries. It's the same when you make that effort with executive buyers.

Don't be afraid to use new terminology, even if you aren't an expert on the subject. You will learn. In the meantime, you can change the conversation and get the attention of more, and more powerful, decision makers. The bottom line is, these are just people trying to get by and do their jobs the best they can, and if you can help them, they will listen. If you have a solution that solves their specific problem, they will want to talk to you. Make the effort to discover the company's goals, find out who the buyers are, learn their initiatives that support those goals, and understand how each buyer measures success. With this knowledge, you can craft a message that resonates with those stakeholders and their respective lines of business.

We hope this chapter has helped you think more deeply about aligning your solutions and your sales tactics not just to specific industries or businesses but, at a very granular level, to specific buyers within businesses. There are many stakeholders for complex deals, so it's imperative to take the time to understand how your solution impacts the company and its various lines of business. Understanding different buyers' key initiatives and performance indicators will allow you to speak their language, not yours. Doing so will give you the confidence and some starting points to have conversations with people outside of your comfort zone.

If you get a handle on the goals, metrics, opportunities, and challenges your customer faces—and align them with what your solutions can offer—you will suddenly have a much more compelling and intelligent-sounding conversation with your buyers. Doing this for your many deals may seem overwhelming, but the more conversations you have, the more you'll learn and the easier it will be to sound like you know what you're talking about. Because you will! Funny how that works.

LINE OF BUSINESS INSIGHTS BEST PRACTICES

The average number of stakeholders involved in a deal has doubled from just a few years ago. As a seller, you have to consider not only your champion in the deal but all the other decisions makers across the company's lines of business. Insight-Led Selling's best practices will help you better engage with these buyers, address their specific interests and concerns, and gain a wider audience of approval for your solution.

- Put yourself in your buyers' shoes. Every stakeholder wants to know "what's in it for me?" so you have to be prepared to answer that question—before they ask it. Your solution will appeal to buyers for different reasons, and there is no one sales pitch that sells everyone.

- Know the most common goals, trends, risks, and opportunities among each line of business in an industry, then discover which ones your stakeholders are experiencing.

- Learn the company's goals and strategies and how each stakeholder's initiatives support them. Know their KPIs, too, and how to talk about them in their line of business language.

- Identify the "alphas" or the top decision makers. Appeal to them, find common ground among all the stakeholders, and build a coalition of support. Turn that momentum into a consensus.

- Pay attention to any red flags from the stakeholders. Politics and hidden agendas exist in every company and garnering the support of key influencers doesn't guarantee the sale. Don't be afraid to ask the hard questions required to uncover the unspoken objections to your solution.

FINANCIAL INSIGHTS

"A seller should know my company's financial performance. Before they try to sell me something, they have to understand my financial position and what's going on in the company's business functions that could impact it. A seller who knows the financials knows what I'm focused on right now."

—CANDY CONWAY, former VP, Global Operations, AT&T

When we talk to salespeople about finance, we like to start the conversation with the question "How many of you took finance in school?"

Half the people raise their hand. Then we ask, "How many of you liked it?"

Every hand goes down.

If you don't love finance, you're not alone. Yet, managing financial performance is one of the most important responsibilities of executives.

Financial insight into your customers' performance provides crucial benefits:

- Helps you think like executive buyers do, seeing their needs and your offering from their perspective

- Highlights the strengths and weaknesses of their financial performance so you can better identify their pain points and areas of opportunity to improve

- Provides insights into where your solution potentially adds the greatest value

In a FinListics survey of sellers, shown in Figure 4-1, 23 percent said they feel comfortable talking about it, while 32 percent believe they're making some progress on that front, and *45 percent* believe their understanding needs significant improvement.6

The good news is that what executives want to know often has little to do with what you learned in class. Whether you love it or hate it, learning about finance from an executive's point of view will cure you of any "finance fears" and introduce you to powerful insight.

Your customer is driven by revenue growth, profitability, and utilization of assets. Insight-Led Selling helps you look at their performance and gain perspective that will help you have a better conversation and better align with their goals. You can also identify areas where your solutions will potentially help them. Insight and being able to talk about their financial performance are critical to selling up the ladder.

---

6   Stephen Timme, "Curing Sellers' Fear of Finance," Forbes, March 18, 2020, https://www.forbes.com/sites/forbesbusinessdevelopmentcouncil/2020/03/18/curing-sellers-fear-of-finance/#17cfac666149.

Figure 4-1. How Well Does Your Sales Force Understand Their Customer's Financial Performance?

FINANCIAL LANGUAGE

At the end of the day, businesses exist to make money. What do they do with that money? They maintain the existing organization, but they also use it to grow, hire people, and help their community. Companies have to make a profit, though startup companies typically get a pass on this for some period of time.

Publicly traded companies need to return value to shareholders to maintain investment. Non-publicly traded companies also focus on profits so that they, like public companies, can grow the business, invest in their people, and so forth.

In other words, if you're working with businesses, no matter what kind, you have to be thinking about money, because that's what it's all about. You can talk about all kinds of solutions, but if they won't help grow revenue, increase profits, or result in higher utilization of assets, you won't find much interest.

In thinking about financial impacts, the numbers tell a story. As you research a company, if there's a big change in any of the financial metrics, positive or negative, it'll jump out at you. You can then dig in to figure out what's happening. Maybe there was a change in product/service mix or a security breach. Maybe they acquired another company. Maybe they've had to take a huge write-off or introduced a new, wildly successful product. Doing your homework helps you understand a company's financial story.

Finance is the common language of business. People in product development have to explain to senior executives how a new product impacts the top line and how it meets needs in the market. Marketing wants to spend hundreds of millions, if not billions, of dollars on coming up with clever campaigns. In order to justify that investment, they have to explain the impact on revenue and profit. IT wants to migrate to the cloud, which has technology benefits, but at the end of the day, they also need to explain how doing so reduces costs, supports growth initiatives, and ultimately increases revenue.

The list goes on and on and on. Each line of business has its own metrics and language, but when they all get together in an executive meeting, they'll speak in the context of finance: grow the top line, better manage expenses, and get better utilization of assets. That's how they communicate with each other, and when you communicate with them, you also need to be able to explain how your solution will enhance overall financial performance.

CURING SELLERS' FEAR OF FINANCE

When Stephen was a college professor, Introduction to Finance was a required course. One student, who hadn't been doing very well, came into Stephen's office in his last semester. When asked why in the world he waited until the final semester of his degree program to take what was known as the hardest core course, he said, "I was kind of hoping you guys would drop it."

He wasn't alone in fearing finance or thinking the subject isn't helpful or fun. However, there's a lot more to finance than numbers and equations that might seem to have no place in the seller's workplace. If, like Stephen's student, you're simply afraid of the topic, it's time to face that fear head-on. Embracing finance could be the single most powerful step you will ever take in advancing your selling success.

Ideally, companies should adopt an initiative for helping "cure" the finance fears of everyone involved in sales including solutions architects, industry experts, and so on. The fastest and most dramatic results are achieved by making it a group effort. Our six-step process takes advantage of the research you've done in the previous three chapters. This builds on the Chapter 2 concepts of knowing your industry roadmap and Chapter 3 knowing your buyers' goals, strategies, and initiatives. Let's look at the steps to curing sellers' fear of finance shown in Figure 4-2. Then we'll step through an application of the process in action.

> *"An ideal situation is one where the seller knows our financial performance. Who wouldn't love for a vendor to be able to have that conversation? For publicly traded companies, almost all the information they need is out there. Think about how powerful it would be to have a seller start the discussion with something like, 'We know you're building profit margin on price increases and that your volume is flat. Here's how we can get you to a more sustainable model with cost improvements as well.'*
>
> *"Unfortunately, I know very few sellers who are equipped to have this kind of conversation."*
>
> **—DAWN GARIBALDI,** President, Amplify Strategy, and former Vice-President, Supply Chain, Fabric & Home Care–Asia, Procter & Gamble

Step 1: Identify Key Areas of Performance

In this step, you're laying the foundation with an industry outside-in perspective, identifying at a very high level the three things the buyer cares about the most. You're essentially answering the question, "What are the two or three areas of performance that drive the majority of the company value?" These measures vary by industry, but for all industries, a common key area is *revenue growth*. Figure 4-3 illustrates the financial drivers for what we call goods and services companies, which includes industries such as manufacturing, retail, oil and

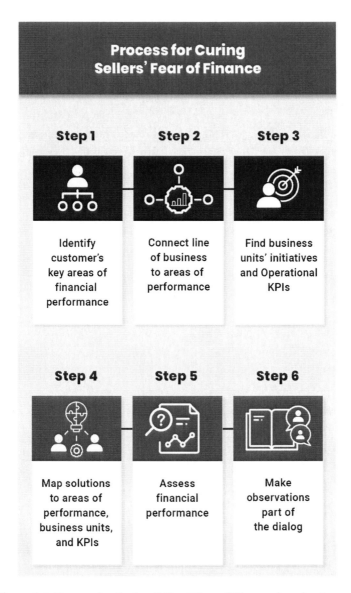

Figure 4-2. Process for Curing Sellers' Fear of Finance is a six-step method that every employer can use to ease sellers into conversations that leverage financial information for more, bigger, and better deals.

gas, telecommunications, and business services. See the Chapter 2 section in the appendix for financial drivers for banking and insurance. Revenue growth is a key driver for all industries. For a retailer, *Operating Income Margin and Days in Inventory* are two of the three key areas, and for a system integrator, the focus is on *selling, general and administrative,* and *Days Sales Outstanding.* For oil and gas, two of the areas are Cost of Goods Sold and Fixed Asset Utilization.

It all starts with some measure of overall performance, such as a return measure or earnings per share. Overall performance breaks into three different areas, as shown in Figure 4-3.

REVENUE

First, how fast is the top-line revenue growing? For a manufacturer, you'd look at product price and service contracts. For retail, how much merchandise did they sell, and how much did they get in extended warranty revenue? As we saw in Chapter 2, revenue growth varies across industries. Software tends to experience double-digit growth, whereas utilities often grow less than 1 percent.

PROFITABILITY

The next component is some measure of profitability. Profits are the amount of revenue that you have, less the costs associated with generating that revenue. When we look at profits relative to revenue, we call that profitability. Remember the discussion in Chapter 2 where we discussed that one of the drivers of prof-

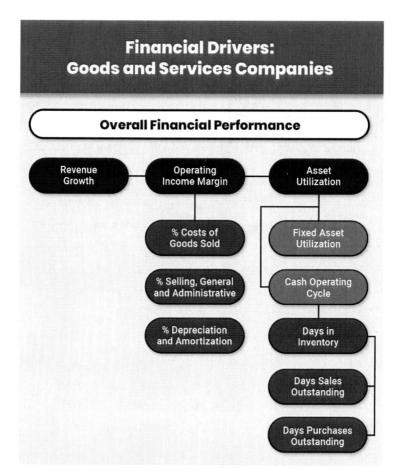

Figure 4-3. Financial Drivers: Goods and Services Companies.

itability is the value a company delivers to its customer. Pharmaceutical companies have a very high profit margin at over 20 percent. They deliver lifesaving medication. Wholesale companies' profit margin is less than 4 percent. They add value, of course, but not as much as a pharmaceutical company.

For a lot of companies, one of the biggest costs associated with making products or delivering services is Cost of Goods Sold (COGS), which may represent 50–70 percent of their revenue. For retail, COGS includes items such as merchandise, store, and logistics costs. COGS for a service company primarily includes the labor to provide services. Manufacturing COGS includes items such as materials, labor, overhead, and logistics.

Another major cost bucket for a lot of companies is Selling, General and Administrative (SG&A), which includes sales expenses, marketing expenses, finance and accounting, IT, HR, legal, and so on. Like COGS, it varies by industry and often represents 15–30 percent of revenue. SG&A tends not to absorb as much revenue as COGS, but it's still significant and companies are always looking at ways to better manage it.

Asset Utilization

You got the revenue and profit pieces. But guess what? Companies need to invest in assets to generate revenue and profits. This investment is broken into two main categories:

- Fixed Asset Utilization

- Cash Operating Cycle

Fixed assets include investments in IT assets such as infrastructure (although this investment is decreasing with cloud services). A manufacturer needs production facilities and distribution assets. Retailers and wholesale distributors need distribution centers and, at times, stores. An electric utility invests in generation, transmission, and distribution assets. Oil and gas invest in production assets such as on- and offshore oil rigs and refining facilities. An airline invests in aircraft and passenger gates. You need to look at how well a company is utilizing its fixed assets. Are they generating a lot of revenue or little revenue?

Fixed Asset Utilization is a measure of how much a company generates in revenue compared to its investment in fixed assets. A company has $100 million in fixed assets and $200 million in revenue. Fixed Asset Utilization is 2.00, meaning that a dollar invested in fixed assets generates $2.00 in revenue throughout the year.

Fixed Asset Utilization is impacted by how capital intensive is the industry the customer competes and how efficiently they are utilized. In Chapter 3, we talked about wholesale distribution having low capital intensity investing on average $0.10 in fixed assets such as distribution centers per dollar of revenue. Utilities is one of the most capital intensive, investing around $3.00 in assets such as generation plants, transmission, and distribution assets per $1.00. Another capital-intensive industry is mining that on average invests $1.00 in fixed asset (mines and mining equipment) per $1.00 in revenue.

FIXED ASSET UTILIZATION

FIXED ASSET UTILIZATION IS A measure of how much a company generates in revenue compared to its investment in fixed assets. Say a company has $100 million in fixed assets and $200 million in revenue. Fixed Asset Utilization is 2.00, meaning that $1.00 invested in fixed assets generates $2.00 in revenue throughout the year. Fixed Asset Utilization is heavily dependent on how capital intensive an industry is. Globally, large telecommunications companies generate almost $1.20 in revenue for $1.00 invested in fixed asset. The better performers are closer to $1.60. Most companies are constantly seeking ways to improve the utilization of fixed assets and improve overall financial performance.

Then there's the Cash Operating Cycle. The Cash Operating Cycle provides a measure of how quickly a company converts its investment in inventory into cash. It consists of the following:

- **Days in Inventory:** Days a company has invested in inventory

- **Days Sales Outstanding:** Days a company takes to receive payment from customers

- **Days Purchases Outstanding:** Days a company takes to pay suppliers

Executives focus on the Cash Operating Cycle since it is a major driver of cash flow, which is one of the most important contributors to a company's market value and access to funds.

CASH OPERATING CYCLE

CASH OPERATING CYCLE IS THE net number of days a company has invested in inventory, accounts receivable, and accounts payable. For example, for large global automotive parts manufacturers the average Cash Operating Cycle is 44 days, which comprises 48 days in inventor plus 55 days in Days Sales Outstanding less 59 days in Days Purchases Outstanding. The better performers' Cash Operating Cycle is at –2 days! How do they have a negative Cash Operating Cycle? Days in Inventory is 35 days and Days Sales Outstanding at 47 days, both of which are lower than the average performer which is a good thing. Days Purchase Outstanding is 84 days compared to the average performers' 59 days. One of the biggest contributors the better performers' –2 days is they lean more heavily on their suppliers.

Many companies are continually working on ways to lower Days in Inventory and Days Sales Outstanding and increase Days Purchases Outstanding. How many of your customers are constantly asking for longer credit terms?

Step 2: Connect Lines of Business to Areas of Performance

Now, you may be tempted to immediately show your customer how you can help them. Wait. Instead, first figure out whom to call on and which of the two or three areas they're aligned with at a high level. In other words, answer the question, *Whom do I sell to?* Figure 4-4 maps Areas of Financial Performance to the buyers who care about them. Use this as a guide to determine which buyers would be most interested in your solution. Sellers often tell us that using this helps finding new buyers in a company.

By this point, you know whom you're selling to. Start thinking about how they view financial performance. Very few buyers are interested in all the different Areas of Financial Performance. If you're selling to customer service, marketing, or sales, they're most interested in managing revenue or revenue growth. Also, since those units are a part of SG&A, they're very conscious of those associated costs as well. They're not as interested in utilization of assets.

The operations function in manufacturing, on the other hand, will be very concerned about the cost of running those facilities, the Cost of Goods Sold, the materials, the labor, and the overhead. They also want to optimize the utilization manufacturing facilities, which has a direct impact on Fixed Asset Utilization.

Many other buyer functions and metrics could be in play, and we won't list them all here. The takeaway is, whom are you talking to, and what do they care about?

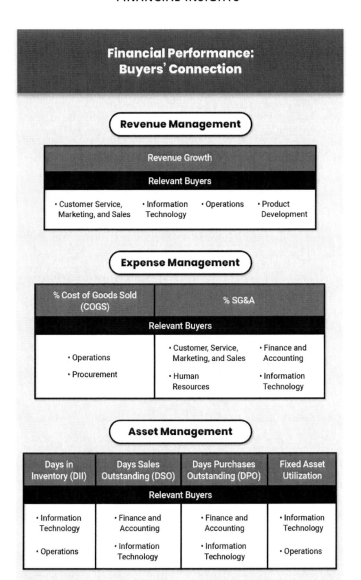

Figure 4-4. Financial Performance Buyers' Connection. Know which buyers are focused on the different Areas of Financial Performance.

TALKING THE TALK OPENS THE DOOR

A SALES REP AT ONE of our clients typically calls into her customers at the plant level. In one of our workshops, she shared that the conversations focus on run speed, Capacity Utilization, and so on because that's what plant managers get paid to worry about. After the workshop, she did some research and met with a plant manager again. This time, she told him she'd noticed their Cost of Goods Sold was trending upward. She didn't get into a lot of detail or even mention any numbers, but the plant manager immediately noted that he'd just received information from his CFO on that metric, and it was of great interest to the business unit. He directed her several levels up in the organization to speak with someone about it.

The point is, you don't necessarily need deep financial knowledge to reach an alpha buyer or the person who sets the budget. You simply need to speak their language and be able to connect the dots between what they care about and what you have to offer. Before you walk into a meeting, remember this: Just like you should dress for the job you want, you should talk like the person you want to talk to.

As we've said, finance is the common language of business, so using the right words matters. Numbers can be scary, but we're here to help you with that fear. It's also possible to have a financial or business conversation without talking about a number at all. Dropping in "Cost of Goods Sold" or "Fixed Asset Utilization" with the right person at the right time can suddenly get you bumped up to the alpha buyer, where you want to be. Know which metrics your buyer cares about and speak to them accordingly.

Step 3: Find Business Units' Initiatives and Operational KPIs

In order to map your solutions, you need to look for priorities and pain points from the buyer's perspective and then figure out how what you offer maps to those areas.

Maybe the answer to the question in step 2 is Marketing. Okay, what does Marketing care about? Growing the top line. They're aligned with revenue and looking at metrics such as campaign success rates and cross-sell/upsell.

Or if you're selling Internet of Things (IoT) for industrial, whom are you selling to? The COO. COOs care about direct costs, unplanned capacity, and utilization of their assets.

What if you're in banking? If you sell to the chief risk officer, what do they care about? The cost, risk, compliance, and so forth.

In Chapter 3, we showed you examples of Operational KPIs by different business units, and again in Figure 4-5, you can see how this information plays into step 3 in curing a seller's fear of finance.

You don't have to know all the answers rights away. For one, you can ask questions of your customer and view investor presentations that point you toward concepts to research in more detail. Also, as we said, this is group therapy, a team

How Is Success Measured?

Marketing

- Number of campaigns
- Response rate
- Price optimization
- Cross-sell/up-sell
- New customers

Information Technology

- Application development expense
- Application management expense
- IT spend per employee
- Return on IT investment
- Projects delivered on time/on budget

Customer Care

- Net Promoter Score
- Customer retention
- First-time resolution
- Customer satisfaction by channel
  (web chat, IVR, service rep, etc.)

Human Resources

- Employee satisfaction
- Employee turnover
- Cost of recruiting, development, and retention

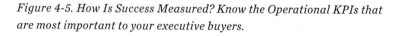

Figure 4-5. How Is Success Measured? Know the Operational KPIs that are most important to your executive buyers.

effort—enlist your colleagues and resources. This process starts you thinking at a very high level. Don't get into detail. Just answer the questions, *whom are you selling to?, and to the best of your ability, what do they really care about?*

Step 4: Map Your Solutions to Areas of Performance and KPIs

Once you know what they care about, what is it that you do? If you sell customer insights or IoT for industrial, what areas of performance are you going to impact? How does the buyer measure those impacts? Remember, this is a group exercise. It requires participation from marketing, industry experts, and sales. It may seem like a lot of work initially—and it can be— but it's well worth the effort. The good news is, doing the work provides a scalable, repeatable process, which experience shows leads to larger deal sizes and sales.

WHICH METRICS DO YOU IMPACT?

There are a lot of metrics in the mix, and you might feel overwhelmed. However, your solution likely impacts only two or three of them. In the six-step therapeutic process, you and your team work to find out which are most relevant and map your offerings to those metrics.

For example, if you're selling a supply chain service, it will influence Cost of Goods Sold. Or if you sell customer insights that can help a retailer do a better job of understanding customer preferences, your solution is all about revenue growth. If you sell technology that helps the IoT—the connectivity of assets in a manufacturing context—you impact Fixed Asset Utilization.

So again, we encourage you to pick two, maybe three of these at most, and develop a deep insight of how your solutions impact those. You don't have to know everything about the business; you're just trying to set yourself apart from the vast majority of sellers who walk through the door.

Step 5: Assess Financial Performance

Once you've got all this valuable knowledge about the industry and customer, it's time to assess the financial performance. This step comes late in the process because you have to look at the performance in the context of whom you're selling to and the company's goals. You can't just look at the numbers and wait for divine inspiration; you need to know what they mean.

For revenue growth, the VP of Sales is thinking about things such as sales attainment, closure rate, and pipeline and how they are impacting growth. Marketing looks at things such as campaign response rate and return on marketing investment—how many dollars of revenue are generated for each dollar invested in marketing and how they are contributing to the top line.

Now let's look at Cost of Goods Sold. The COO, for example, might look at trends in Cost of Goods Sold and wonder about changes in materials, overhead, and labor costs. COVID increased cost per unit because of new protocols and lower

Capacity Utilization. Distribution and Logistics would look at trends in Cost of Goods Sold and think, for example, about how changes in outbound transportation because of shorter delivery times are impacting these costs. Or how a shortage of skilled labor is driving up warehousing costs. The point is, when analyzing an area for financial performance, view it from your buyer's perspective to not only develop more empathy but also better communicate how your solution can help.

We want to teach you the process of conducting an assessment, but more importantly, how you use those insights with your buyers. Remember, a lot of factors go into these metrics. Try looking at them from your buyer's perspective.

In looking at the trends from the buyer's perspective, you can get a lot of insight from what publicly traded companies say. When companies publish their financial reports, they have a section titled something like "Management Discussion and Analysis." In this section, they provide information on the key factors contributing to changes in performance.

The website Seeking Alpha provides a great resource for reading full transcripts of shareholder calls, which include pointed questions for analysts trying to figure out whether a stock is a buy. Management needs to answer to shareholders regarding delivering value, and they'll try to put as positive a spin as possible on whatever's happening, whereas analysts don't have that interest. You can tell which questions management is and isn't comfortable answering. Sometimes they'll slip, get frustrated, or say something off the cuff, revealing much more than their prepared remarks. The numbers tell a story, and the conversation can help you figure out what the real story is.

GROSS PROFIT MARGIN

GROSS PROFIT MARGIN IS GROSS profit, which is revenue less Cost of Goods Sold, expressed as a percentage of revenue. Executives often talk about changes in pricing and product mix when discussing changes in Gross Profit Margin. They focus on Gross Profit Margin because it is an indicator of how well a company is managing all Operational KPIs related to sales—for example, pricing and product development—and Cost of Goods Sold—for example, labor and materials. The average Gross Profit Margin for large software companies in North America is almost 80 percent and for the better performers, 85 percent. By comparison, the average Gross Profit Margin for large manufacturers in North America is around 35 percent.

A couple of years ago, a retailer had some growth, but their Gross Profit Margin had dropped, which is a big deal. On an earnings call, an analyst asked what caused it to drop. Management hemmed and hawed and finally said, "Well, we changed our mix of products." The analyst asked what else they'd done besides making that change, and then they said, "Well, we made some investments in pricing." The analyst wasn't rude, but he asked, "Investment in pricing? What does that mean? You lowered prices; isn't that what you're really saying?"

If you learn this kind of information from a call, as a seller you can say you might not be able to help directly, say, with the lower pricing part, but you sell distribution logistics services that help lower costs elsewhere when prices erode, protecting margins—what we refer to as yin and yang selling. Knowing your buyer's financial trends can help you identify bad ones and figure out ways to compensate.

INSIGHT-LED SELLING IN ACTION

Action: Identify Areas of Financial Performance improved by your solutions

Purpose: Link your solutions to improved financial performance

Use the Financial Drivers Map in Figure 4-3 if you sell to companies such as manufacturing, retail, and business services to help you complete this exercise.

1. Select two to three Areas of Financial Performance that your solutions can improve.

2. What are some of the challenges your customers face when trying to improve in these areas that your solutions help with?

3. In nontechnical terms, create an elevator pitch explaining how your solutions help improve each area of performance.

4. What case studies support how your solutions help improve financial performance in these areas?

Step 6: Make Observations
Part of the Dialog

When you address that primary concern, you'll make it a natural part of the dialog—not give them a financial history lesson. You won't throw around a bunch of jargon or numbers out of context. Instead, you'll speak in terms of relative performance, perhaps saying something like the following:

> *In preparing for this meeting, I reviewed your financial performance. I noticed that Cost of Goods Sold as a percentage of revenue has been trending upward. I read in the management discussion analysis that the trend partly relates to higher materials and labor costs. This helped me understand your goal of improving operational efficiencies to reduce Cost of Goods Sold. I'd like to share with you how we have worked with others in your industry to reduce these costs.*

If you simply dive into the numbers with a statement like, "Your Days in Inventory went from fifty days to sixty-five days," you risk the buyer saying, "Yeah, I know," and tuning out. It's like telling someone they're ten pounds overweight when what they really want to hear is how to get in shape. By contrast, contextualizing the raw numbers and aligning them to a tailored solution tells executives something they don't already know, why they should care, *and* what you can help them do about it. As a result, you shift the focus from price to the value of your solutions.

Pointing out those trends in a respectful, solution-oriented way—and without trying to sound like a know-it-all—

will get results. Speak on subjects outside your wheelhouse can feel uncomfortable at first, but if you have a way to help buyers achieve their goals, they'll want to hear it. They're not antsy to buy your product; they're antsy for *results*. It's like if someone came to you, as a seller, and said they could help you shatter your quota, you'd want to listen.

CASE STUDY: APPLYING THE CURING SELLERS' FEAR OF FINANCE PROCESS

Now let's apply the six steps to curing sellers' fear of finance. Your customer is a department store retailer selling women's, men's, and children's clothing. It has $20 billion in revenue and over a thousand stores. Like many brick-and-mortar retailers, it has struggled to grow revenue and maintain profitability because of changes in consumer buying behavior and the "Amazon Effect."

But your customer is fighting back. It has two key goals:

- Drive revenue growth

- Expand profit margin

You offer solutions that help deliver greater customer insights in retail. So you focus on the drive revenue growth goal.

You know from Chapter 3 the next question is, "What are the strategies and initiatives for achieving the goal?" You review financial reports and investor presentations, listen in on the earnings call, and identify the following strategy and initiatives that align with your solutions' capabilities.

Strategy: Enhance Loyalty and Value Initiatives:

- Best-in-class rewards program

- Drive productivity through deeper engagement

- Deliver personalized experiences

- Let's begin the six-step process.

Step 1: Identify Customer's Key Areas of Financial Performance

For retail, three of the key Areas of Financial Performance are:
- Revenue Growth

- Operating Income Margin

- Days in Inventory

Step 2: Connect Lines of Business to Areas of Performance

For retail, some of the business units connected to all three Areas of Financial Performance are:

- Merchandising

- Marketing

- Distribution and logistics

- Store operations

You know these are some of the connected lines of business because these are some of the areas retail executives talk about in investor presentations and on earnings calls.

Step 3: Find Lines of Business's Initiatives and Operational KPIs

The next step in the process is to identify the lines of business's initiatives and Operational KPIs. Examples of these initiatives and KPIs for the four lines of business identified above are shown in Figure 4-6. Note that this is not an exhaustive list but provided for illustrative purposes.

During this step, you think, "Which one of these initiatives and KPIs can my solutions help better manage?" Hold on, we will talk about this in step 4. Also, we often hear that by completing step 3, sellers find new buyers to talk to.

Step 4: Map Solutions to Areas of Performance, Lines of Business, and KPIs

This is one of the most important steps since buyers want to know how your solutions improve their KPIs and ultimately how much are the financial benefits. Again, you sell solutions that improve customer insights.

Marketing is probably whom you usually engage with

Business Function	Initiatives	Operational KPIs
Examples of Initiatives and Operational KPIs for LOBs Aligned with Driving Revenue Growth		
Merchandising	• Match product assortment with regional demand/localization • Expand private brands/labels	• Sell-through rate • Average transaction value • Markdowns
Marketing	• Use analytics to tailor messaging, special offers, and online/mobile displays • Create marketing campaigns for new online channels across physical and digital media	• Campaign response rate • Customer churn • Marketing expense
Distribution and Logistics	• Expand delivery options: home, BOPIS, BORIS, buy online, distribute from store • Track orders in real time and provide advance shipping notice	• Orders delivered on time • Customer order cycle time • Logistics costs
Store Operations	• Offer 'endless aisle' kiosk to order items out of stock • Improve pickup desk performance	• Comparable store sales • Sales per employee • Sales per square foot

Figure 4-6. Examples of Initiatives and Operational KPIs for Retail LOBs Aligned with Driving Revenue Growth.

since all marketing KPIs could be improved and will help achieve the goal of driving revenue. But what about the goal of increasing profitability? More effective marketing campaigns mean for the same marketing budget, revenue will be higher. Ready for this? This means that marketing expense would be lower as a percentage of revenue and, all else the same, profitability increases. So when talking to marketing, you could talk about how your solutions help contribute to the goals of revenue growth and profitability.

Merchandising should also be interested since having greater insights would improve all of that line of business's KPIs. It would also help improve profitability since there should be fewer markdowns. And by buying merchandise that is more aligned with customer demand, Days in Inventory should be lowered.

But what about store operations? Note that some of store operations KPIs are based on revenue or sales. Store operations would not likely be the direct buyer of your solution, but they likely would be part of the village of buyers. Remember in Chapter 3 we talked about "it takes a village"? By showing how your solutions could help improve some of their KPIs, they could become an advocate of your solution.

You may have never thought about talking to Distribution and Logistics if you sell solutions that improve customer insight. Here's how you can help. One of their KPIs is Days in Inventory and we have already talked about improving Days in Inventory. Also, with great customer insights, inventory can be better stocked and positioned to reduce customer order cycle time and increase Orders Delivered On Time. Distribution and Logistics may not be the main buyer of your solution, but just like store operations, by showing how your solutions can help improve their KPIs, they likely will recommend your solutions.

Like we have said before, an important takeaway from this step is better insight into your usual buyers, while also finding new buyers.

Step 5: Assess Financial Performance

Now you are ready to assess the customer's financial performance. Steps 1–4 provide a good perspective on the assessment of performance. Also, remember the purpose of conducting this assessment is to help you better understand the motivation for the customer's goals, strategies, and initiatives, better communicate with buying executives, and differentiative yourself from the competition.

You are looking for how the company is performing over time and how it compares to its peers and industry. You do not need to get into a lot of details. Keep it high level. We recommend that you refer to the customer's trend in performance over time and performance relative to their peers.

This is a good example of using reference to relative performance with an executive buyer. One of our customers' sellers was talking to an executive at a major medical insurance company. The company's profit margin had been dropping in part due to changes in healthcare legislation and mix of insurance policies. The seller knew that a goal was to increase profitability by improving operational efficiencies, which was a sweet spot for the seller's solutions. The seller asked the executive about the goal and initiatives and how they were going. She next referred to noticing that SG&A expenses as a percentage of revenue were trending up and was a main contributor to the decline in overall profitability. Notice she did not get into all the details such as, "Your percentage SG&A has gone from a low of 20.3 percent and is now much higher at 24.8 percent!" Way too nerdy. She shared with us that the executive was very surprised that she knew this, and they had a good conversation about how the seller's solutions could potentially help better manage SG&A.

Assessing financial performance goes beyond just the number. A critical part is investigating what management is saying about their performance which, as we noted earlier, is included in the Management Discussion and Analysis in their financial filings. Our experience is that sellers are often amazed at the amount of information that is publicly available about a customer's financial performance. And the insights that are provided help sellers to better know the customer's business and show how their solutions fit into the bigger picture. Unfortunately, very few sellers take the time to review this information. In our interviews, many executives believed that only 10–20 percent of sellers have this information. So set yourself apart from the competition and spend the time to see what management is talking about.

Figure 4-7 shows that assessing a customer's financial performance is a five-step process. As you are conducting this assessment, answer these questions:

- How does this year compare to previous years?

- Is there a trend?

- What is management talking about?

- How do they compare to peers and industry?

- Is there an overall trend for the customer, peers, and industry?

OVERALL PERFORMANCE

There are many different measures of financial performance. The two areas we recommend you review are:

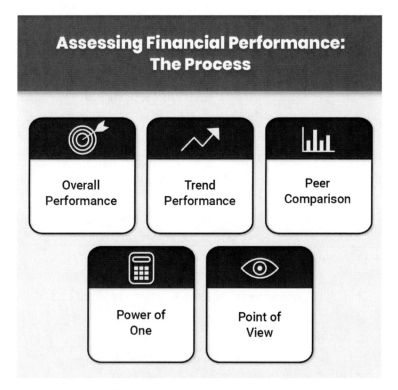

Figure 4-7. Assessing Financial Performance: The Process.

- Revenue growth

- Profitability

Earlier, we talked about why these two areas are so important to senior executives and investors. Regardless of measure of overall performance such as Return on Capital or Earnings per Share, revenue growth and profitability are two of the most important drivers.

When reviewing revenue growth and profitability, some items to consider are changes in:

- Pricing strategy

- Product mix

- Operating expenses

- Customer buying behavior

- Overall economic activity

REVENUE GROWTH

Figure 4-8A shows the customer revenue growth over the last five years. It shows that this year's performance is the lowest in five years and there is a declining trend over time and now the customer is losing revenue. That is never a good thing!

Figure 4-8A also shows what we call the Value of the Gap.

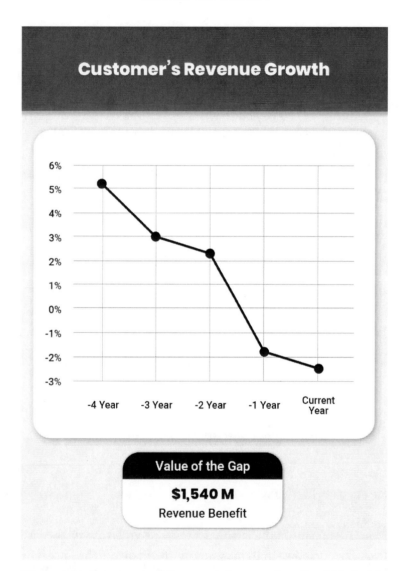

Figure 4-8A. Assessment of Customer's Revenue Growth, which, in this example, is dropping over time. Source: FinListics ClientIQ.

This is the revenue benefit if the customer could go from the current year to the best year's performance. The value of the gap is $1,540 million. A lot of companies perform this type of analysis. It helps put the percentage revenue growth in a better perspective. The gap of $1,540 million is substantial and provides insights into why the customer is working so hard to improve performance.

Looking at the company's revenue growth, you can speculate why it is dropping. But why speculate? Let's see what management is talking about by reviewing their comments in the Management Discussion and Analysis in their financial filings. They first reference that comparable store sales have been negative. Comparable store sales is the year-over-year growth at individual stores. What's causing the drop in comparable store sales? They talk about fewer customers visiting the stores, and when they do, the average value of transactions at checkout is dropping. They also talk about the fact that online sales increased in the low double-digits. Despite the growth in online sales, year-over-year continues to decline.

Knowing what management is talking about provides valuable insights into what is top of mind. You can start thinking about how your solutions, for example, could increase average value of transactions or accelerate online sales. Perhaps you can't do anything about increasing the number of customers visiting stores since this reflects a shift in buying behavior. But you could reference how your solution boosts sales through other channels to help offset the lower store foot traffic.

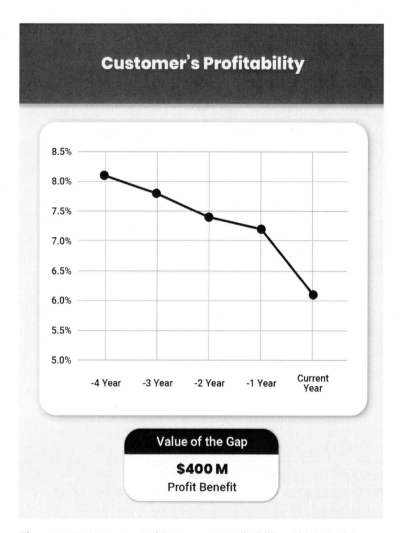

Figure 4-8B. Assessment of Customer's Profitability, which, in this example, is decreasing year over year. Source: FinListics ClientIQ.

Profitability

Figure 4-8B shows profitability performance. Profitability is measured by the Operating Income Margin. Remember from Chapter 1, Operating Income Margin is Operating Income (revenue less all operating costs such as cost of goods; selling, general and administrative; and depreciation) expressed as a percentage of revenue. Like revenue growth, this year's performance is the lowest in five years; it is declining over time. The value of the gap is $400 million, which is quite a lot. For profitability, the value of the gap is the increase in Operating Income by returning best year's performance. Again, companies often conduct this type of analysis since it shows in dollars the benefits of improving performance. Some areas management highlighted for the decline in profitability are higher shipping costs due to more online sales with faster deliveries, markdowns, and labor costs. Remember that your customer insights solutions can't help the customer better manage higher shipping and labor costs, but you would want to explore how they could better manage markdowns.

Your assessment of the customer's overperformance is that it looks anemic, which it is. But this assessment provides valuable insights into why the client has established strategies and initiatives to enhance performance. It also highlights the need for you to be able to show how your solutions can help improve performance and by how much. It also will help you be more relevant to the customer since you are thinking the same way they are about what urgently needs to be addressed.

Trend Performance and Peer and Industry Comparison

It's now time to assess the Areas of Financial Performance that are most focused on your buyers. This involves analyzing their performance over time compared to their peers and their industry. Since we are focused on marketing, we will stay with revenue growth. If we were targeting, for example, Distribution and Logistics, we would review areas of performance such as percentage Cost of Goods Sold and Days in Inventory since that is where most of those costs are recorded.

We get feedback from sellers all the time about how buyers really appreciate a discussion about how they compare to their peers and industry. Most companies' financial groups conduct this type of analysis. What executives really like is a seller's point of view on why it is different and, ultimately, how it can be improved.

This is one of our favorite stories about using peer and industry performance with an executive. One of our customers provides manufacturing solutions to help lower costs and increase Capacity Utilization. They were calling on a pharmaceutical company and had a meeting with the CFO. The company had a great reputation and, overall, were very well managed. In preparation for the meeting, the seller assessed the customer's performance over time and compared it to its peers in the industry. Revenue growth was excellent, as was profitability. The one area that appeared to be underperforming was Fixed Asset Utilization, which is simply the dollars of revenue generated throughout the year for a dollar invested in fixed assets such as manufacturing facilities.

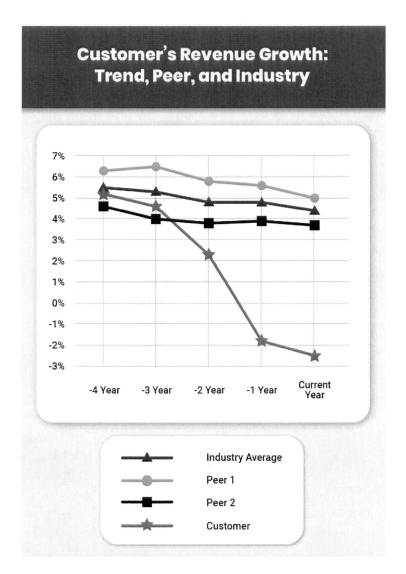

Figure 4-9. Customer's Revenue Growth shows a declining trend in revenue growth for the customer's peers and overall industry, with the customer being the lowest performer. Source: FinListics ClientIQ.

The customer consistently had a lower Fixed Asset Utilization than its peers and industry average. This was shared with the CFO, who seemed surprise. She was a well-respected CFO whom the seller could tell was very smart. They talked about things that might be causing this, such as differences in their therapeutics portfolio since some classes of therapeutics require higher investments in manufacturing assets than others. Also, they talked about perhaps they were building more manufacturing capacity as they continued to expand internationally and they would grow into these facilities, which would increase Fixed Asset Utilization. Our customer shared what they had seen their other customers do operationally to increase Fix Asset Utilization.

It was a great conversation that started with the simple observation that the customer's Fixed Asset Utilization was lower than its peers and industry. Our client was fortunate enough to have the CFO sponsor a meeting with the senior VP of global manufacturing to better understand why there was a difference in utilization, and they eventually closed a deal.

Figure 4-9 shows the customer's trend, peer, and industry performance for revenue growth. Let's look at this from the perspective of a senior marketing executive. The trend performance is the same in overall performance. The customer is the lowest performer in most years. What are some of the factors that might be causing this? Perhaps the customer was a laggard in adopting omnichannel that allows customers to shop how they wanted (in-store and online). You could develop some insights into this by comparing the customer's online sales as a percentage of revenue to its peers and industry average. You could research the customer's policies such as Buy Online and Pick Up in Store or Buy Online and Return in Store. These are retail examples, but the point is, you need to assess your customer's numbers, but you also need to dig deeper to develop insights into some of the contributing factors.

Marketing is not responsible for driving all of revenue growth, but they are a big contributor. For example, if merchandising consistently buys low-demand merchandise and store operations has terrible customer service, marketing can have the most wonderful promotions in the world, but revenue growth is not going to look good.

Now it's time to think like your marketing buyers. What are they thinking about these trends and comparisons? They are thinking they need to quickly find ways to change these or they will be looking for a new place of employment. You have some pretty good ideas about how they want to improve revenue growth performance because you know some of the marketing initiatives you identified earlier from an investor presentation, which were:

- Best-in-class rewards program

- Drive productivity through deeper engagement

- Deliver personalized experiences

Marketing is thinking how implementing each of these initiatives would increase revenue growth and by how much. They also want to know how your solutions can help. Where have you helped customers with similar initiatives? And can you tell them something they don't know such as what the pitfalls are and how they can be avoided?

"From a financial standpoint, companies are looking to make money or save money. Sellers have to decide which of these they can do. They can figure it out by learning their customer's financial performance and their goals, and through their experiences with other companies in the industry. If they can't help the company make or save money, they shouldn't waste their time or the customer's."

—**JIM AUGUST,** VP of Enterprise Architecture at a
Fortune 500 Life Insurance Company

POWER OF ONE

Earlier, we saw that the value of the gap was $1,540 million for revenue growth. This is quite large, and experience shows to close a gap like this often takes strategic initiatives that take multiple years to implement.

The Power of One helps provide insights into the financial benefits of improving areas of performance by 1 percent. We examine the Power of One in more detail in Chapter 5. Like the value of the gap, many companies internally conduct this type of analysis. It helps management better understand the value of even a small incremental change and identify opportunities for the greatest leverage. The Power of One for your customer is $200 million in revenue. Remember the customer has $20 billion in revenue and 1 percent of that is $200 million.

The Power of One is a great conversation starter. The customer did not provide a specific goal around growing revenue. So after you have confirmed marketing's initiatives and share how your solutions have helped others in the industry, you may have a conversation something like this:

"My analysis shows that for your company a 1 percent improvement in revenue adds $200 million in revenue. Does that sound right?"

The answer will be yes since the value is simply 1 percent of the customer's revenue. Since you have likely already built credibility, your next question is:

"What is your goal for improving revenue?"

Let's say the answer is 3 percent. You have just been told that the goal is to improve revenue by $600 million, which is $200 million multiplied by three. You now know the goal. It helps put your solutions' revenue benefits in perspective. If your solutions deliver total benefits of $10 million, they likely are of limited interest. If they can deliver, say, $100 million or more, they likely are of great interest.

POINT OF VIEW

You have assessed the customer's financial performance from the buyer's perspective and now it's time to develop a point of view. The point of view includes:

- Assessment of the customer's overall performance and those areas most relevant to the buyer

- How your solutions align the buyer's initiatives and areas of financial focus

In this application, your assessment of the customer's overall performance is that it is deteriorating and in dire need of improvement. Marketing is most focused on revenue growth, which is declining over time and most times underperforming its peers and industry. Time is of the essence. Investors almost always punish the stock value of companies performing like your customer and change in senior management happens quite often.

You believe your solutions can help. They have helped others in retail with similar marketing and financial goals.

Step 6: Making Observations Part of the Dialog

Now it's time to tie all that you know about the customer together. The dialog with Marketing could look something like this:

> *"My understanding is that one of your company's key goals is to increase revenue growth by pursuing the marketing-focused initiatives offering a best-in-class rewards program, driving deeper customer engagement, and delivering personalized experiences. Are you still pursuing these goals?"*

The answer is yes.

> *"These make sense since I notice your revenue growth has declined over time and on average lower than your peers and industry."*

Notice that you did not provide specific numbers. You don't need to. You just need to refer to trends and relative performance. The buyer will likely be surprised you know this. Most sellers don't.

"I'd like to share with you how our solutions have helped others in retail implement initiatives similar to yours."

Now tell them something they may not know such as the need to address siloed data sources or even that with state-of-the-art technology it won't be very effective if there is a skill gap that needs to be addressed.

Next, share the Power of One and identify the buyer's goal for growth in revenue. What is also very powerful is if you can share with the buyer by how much revenue has increased at your other customers that have purchased your solutions. You would need to make clear that this is not a promise to do the same for the buyer's company.

SUMMARY

Developing insights into a customer's financial performance is essential since managing this performance is one of executives' most important responsibilities. Financial insights empower you to communicate with buyers the way they communicate with each other. This skill helps you identify potential areas of opportunity too. We referenced the Power of One, which shows the financial benefits of improving an area of performance by 1 percent. We explore this in more detail in Chapter 5 since it is a powerful tool for identifying where your solutions add the greatest financial benefits.

FINANCIAL INSIGHTS BEST PRACTICES

Top executives make decisions for one primary reason: to drive business results. That's the bottom line. This is why the more you link financial insights to your proposed solution, the more effective a seller you'll be. Insight-Led Selling best practices will help you get there.

- For your customer, nearly every goal, strategy, initiative, and project is driven by a need to perform financially. Always include high-level financial observations in your initial sales pitch.

- Know their financial performance, but don't criticize it or narrate all the details to them. You are not their company's CFO or even a financial expert, and they already know their numbers better than you do.

- Instead, focus on just one key financial pain point or opportunity area where your solution can create real financial impact.

- Give the buyer a reasonable, conservative estimate of the potential impact of your solution, and do not exaggerate.

- Tell them where your solution has worked and the range of improvement or results that you've seen with other customers.

THE POWER OF ONE

"If you really don't want me to buy your solution, then just show up with a deck of thirty slides and try to walk me through it. I will either ask you to leave, or I'll catch up on my sleep. I will not buy anything.

"Get to the point. Tell me what I need to know. And do it without a slideshow."

—KEN MAY, former CEO, Top Golf, and former COO, Krispy Kreme Doughnuts

Buyers really only care about your solution's business outcomes; no matter how great your features are, buyers want to know how your solution will improve the performance of their business. Since business performance relies heavily on financial performance, you must clearly demonstrate your solution's financial impact, and you should have that conversation as soon as possible.

The problem is, early in the sales cycle, you don't know if you can even help them. Without more information and validation from the client, you can't say, for example, you'll improve profits by 1 percent or 10 percent by improving revenue or lowering expenses. This is where the Power of One can help.

What exactly is the Power of One? The Power of One is the financial benefit from a 1 percent improvement in Areas of Financial Performance or Operational KPIs that are relevant to business units improved by your solutions. For example, say you are talking to Marketing, which we know focuses on the area of financial performance revenue growth and Operational KPIs such as customer churn. We'll get into more details on the subject later in this chapter, but suppose, in this example, the Power of One is $10 million for revenue growth and $2 million for customer retention. We have heard from hundreds of sales professionals that the Power of One is a great conversation starter.

Putting the Power of One to work offers powerful benefits:

1. Provides insights into the greatest areas of leverage for improving performance, which is very useful during account planning

2. Provides a financial focus to your conversation with buyers

3. Offers a way to uncover a buyer's expected business outcomes

The Power of One also helps you communicate with buyers in their language, separates you from competitors, and builds credibility.

Just to be clear about the relationship between Areas of Financial Performance and Operational KPIs, Figure 5-1 shows some of these relationships in the retail industry. Operational KPIs are how companies plan and measure performance. Your solutions deliver financial benefits by helping improve Operational KPIs.

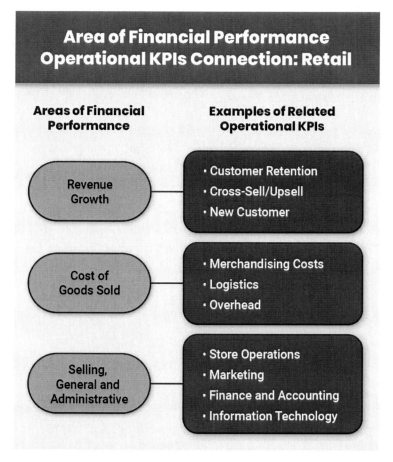

Figure 5-1. Examples of Relationship between Areas of Financial Performance and Operational KPIs for Retail.

We recommend using the Power of One during account planning to identify those KPIs that deliver the greatest benefits. We also recommended using the Power of One in the early stages of the sales process.

A word of caution: Do not position the Power of One as a promise. It's not a proposal or a business case. It is only a conversation starter. Nothing turns a buyer off faster than saying something like, "We can help you and are confident that we could help reduce your SG&A cost by at least 1 percent, which for your company would be at least $60 million." Again, it's simply a conversation starter that sets the cycle on a different tone.

By looking through the Power of One lens before you talk to the customer, you can identify what the buyer is most likely focused on. One of our senior sellers that came on board had worked for a company that extensively used Power of One to talk about the Operational KPIs their solutions could improve. Before meeting with the buyer, she'd go through their list of KPIs to find out which ones provided the biggest benefits. Then she'd ask her solution architect and brand sellers, "What can we do here?" Often, this helped her find new areas to explore with the customer.

HAVING THE CONVERSATION

How do you effectively fit the Power of One into your sales conversations? Figure 5-2 provides the framework for doing this.

Before you get to this point, you need to confirm the company's goals. You might say, for example, "My understanding is you're trying to improve profitability," or, "My understanding is you're trying to improve Days in Inventory. Is that still on the table, or is it now less of a priority?"

If you've done your homework, they'll often answer yes. Alternatively, they might indicate an emerging issue such as COVID has changed the focus, or the key player in a previous initiative has left the company, or they've already solved the problem. First, make sure your proposed target is still a goal.

As we discussed in Chapter 3, once you know the goal, you need to figure out which buyers align with that goal, as well as their associated strategies and Operational KPIs.

After you're clear on those details, share your observations about how other companies have improved in the relevant areas. Ideally, tell the buyer something they don't know. Then talk about how your solutions have helped others in the industry with similar goals, strategies, and initiatives. The CFO at a major retailer would often ask sellers to tell him how their solution helped, then how much it helped. He wanted them to talk in nontechnical terms about how they could help him, and not get into "speeds and feeds."

Once you've laid this groundwork, you'll share the Power of One as a conversation starter with the aim of discovering the client's detailed goals. As we will explore later in this chapter, the Power of One for Areas of Financial Performance is easily tailored to an individual customer since it's based on their reported financial statements. The Power of One for Operational KPIs are typically based on industry averages but scaled to the size of the customer. This is because customers often do not report values of KPIs, say, for cross-sell/upsell, labor, IT spend, Capacity Utilization, and so on. As the sales cycle continues, customers will often share the values for their KPIs.

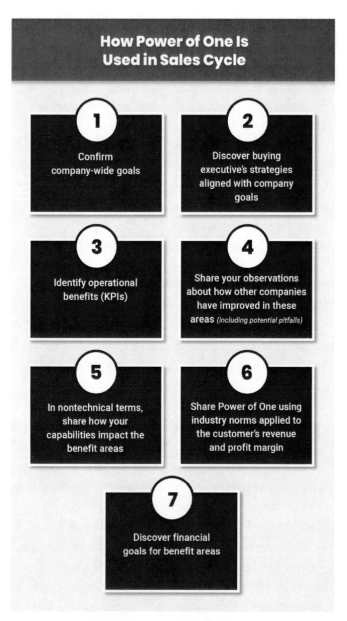

Figure 5-2. How the Power of One Is Used in the Sales Cycle.

As an example, using some industry-based values for IT as a percentage of revenue and applying it to the customer's revenue size, you know that a 1 percent improvement is worth approximately $50 million. The customer has shared with you that this is somewhat close to what a 1 percent improvement would mean for them. They've also shared that they're trying to reduce IT costs by 5 percent, which translates to a goal of $250 million. Knowing all this, you have to bring something big to the table to get their attention.

If you know the relative size of the customer's goal and what a 1 percent improvement would mean in financial benefits, then you can start hypothesizing about your impact. If you get on the same page about goals and numbers, you can start doing some planning regarding delivering that value, all the while asking whether what you're suggesting works for the client.

We recommend picking two or, at most, three key areas to focus on that are of interest to the buyers and that your solutions can potentially improve. You're not trying to memorize a whole list of details and promise specific changes on every level. Rather, you're syncing up your value and solutions relative to the buyer's biggest priorities. If you try to take on too much, you'll lose credibility. The point is to show you've done your homework and can conceptualize value on their scale in a way that's relevant to their expected business outcomes, rather than haggling about price.

However, your solution might, in fact, touch all the metrics of a big, diverse company in some way. In that case, you want to open your aperture, figure out the two or three areas of largest impact, and then focus on those. Some sellers don't really have a big-picture view of their customers. Once they start doing this exercise, they realize what a giant impact they can have. From there, they can come up with a compelling, value-based account plan.

Whatever the details of your solution and industry, you're aligning with the customer: identifying what's important to them and finding the intersection between that focus and what your solution can do. Finally, quantify the potential impact.

> *"Internally, we use a concept like the Power of One. For example, we might apply a 1 percent increase in throughput and look at the impact on cost and profit. So if a seller can show us a 1 percent improvement in throughput, we already know the financial benefits. Maybe they can show us other examples where a 1 percent difference is meaningful to our financial performance and acknowledge we can extrapolate this into our business model. That approach can be a powerful conversation starter and an effective method for a seller to engage with a customer."*

> **—DAWN GARIBALDI,** President, Amplify Strategy, and former Vice-President, Supply Chain, Fabric & Home Care–Asia, Procter & Gamble

POWER OF ONE: AREAS OF FINANCIAL PERFORMANCE

We first explore use of the Power of One for Areas of Financial Performance (e.g., revenue growth) and then how it applies to Operational KPIs such as customer churn and cross-sell/upsell. The Power of One as it relates to Areas of Financial Performance for a goods and services company (e.g., retail, manufacturing, oil and gas, transportation, and business services) includes, among others, items such as:

- **Revenue Growth:** 1 percent improvement in revenue

- **Cost of Goods Sold and Selling, General and Administrative (SG&A):** 1 percent of these expenses' dollar value

- **Days Sales Outstanding and Days in Inventory:** One-day reduction in accounts receivable and inventory, respectively

- **Fixed Asset Utilization:** 1 percent increase utilization of fixed assets

For examples of how the Power of One applies to Areas of Financial Performance for banking and insurance, see the appendix at the end of this book.

Provides insights into the greatest areas of leverage for improving performance

The leverage points vary among industries. In pharmaceuticals, for example, revenue growth will be one of the highest benefits, while Costs of Goods Sold will not. Figure 5-3 illustrates an example of the Power of One for the retail company discussed in Chapter 4:

See the appendix for how these values are calculated. For now, focus on how to use the Power of One and not so much on the calculations. We know from the goals and strategies shown in Chapter 4 that the company is focused on all of these areas of performance. The Power of One shows that the area with one of

Examples of Financial Metric Power of One for Retail Customer

Power of One

Area of Financial Performance	Benefits
Revenue Growth	$200M*
% Cost of Goods Sold	$120M**
% Selling, General and Administrative	$60M**
Days in Inventory	$30M***

*Increase in annual revenue
**Increase in annual profits
***One-time decrease in investment in inventory

Figure 5-3. Examples of Financial Metric Power of One for Retail Customer.

the greatest benefits is Cost of Goods Sold. This would motivate you to think about ways that you could help the company better manage cost of goods even if your focus were, say, helping the company grow revenue or reduce SG&A. This often opens areas to explore further within your company and with the customer.

One of our customers provides world-class data and analytics solutions across a wide range of industries. In pharmaceuticals, their solutions are primarily used in research and development. When R&D goes poorly, it can be a near-total loss, yet when it goes well, it's a moneymaker, driving revenue and profits. This is a good thing since in this industry revenue growth has one of the highest Powers of One because of very high profit margins. But Fixed Asset Utilization also typically has a high Power of One due to the high cost of building bulk manufacturing facilities. Our customer did limited work with pharmaceutical manufacturing, but the Power of One inspired them to think of ways they could help improve performance. The pharmaceutical team talked to their colleagues in other manufacturing industries. The result was, the company developed manufacturing solutions based on experiences with other industries and customized for pharmaceutical, which are now promoted on their website.

INSIGHT-LED SELLING IN ACTION

Action: Apply financial metrics Power of One

Purpose: Identify Areas of Financial Performance where your solutions provide the greatest financial benefits

You can use the FinListics Power of One Value Calculator on www.InsightLedSelling.com, code INSIGHTSELLER, to complete this action.

1. For the two to three Areas of Financial Performance improved by your solutions, what is the Power of One?

2. Based on case studies, what percentage improvement might a customer receive from your solutions? What would be the financial benefit for your customer?

3. How would you use the Power of One in account planning?

4. How would you use the Power of One with the customer? How would it change your conversations with buyers?

Provides a financial focus to your conversation with buyers

The Power of One is an effective way to separate yourself from the competition by adding a financial focus to your conversation. We know from Chapter 4 that one of the retailer's goals is to expand profitability by better managing inventory.

Experience shows that closing significant performance gaps takes much time and change. The Power of One is useful because it shows the value of incremental change while laying the groundwork for more-extensive change.

Let's say you provide Distribution and Logistics solutions that help better manage Days in Inventory by improving inventory visibility. The company has better insights as to where inventory is located—for example, in stores, distribution centers, in transit, and so forth. You are talking to the VP of Distribution and Logistics. In your conversation, you might say that it's your understanding that one of the company's goals is to expand profit margin by better managing inventory. You ask if that's still a top priority, and the VP responds yes. You ask questions about the business unit's initiatives such as improving inventory visibility: how they are proceeding and the challenges. You then share that you understand why there's a focus on better managing inventory since your research shows that profitability has been declining and Days in Inventory has trended upward. At this point, expect the VP to be surprised that you even know this since most sellers don't talk this way. You then share your company's experience with helping lower Days in Inventory. Next, you tell the VP that you have determined that each one-day reduction in Days in Inventory would lower the investment in inventory by $30 million. You ask whether the number sounds about right. The most common response is, "It's pretty close," and it should be since it is based on the customer's published financials.

Offers a way to uncover a buyer's goal for expected financial benefits

The Power of One also helps you discover a client's goal for financial improvement. A lot of companies will provide high-level financial goals such as reduce operating expenses by $500 million or grow revenue by an additional 5 percent, but they leave out details on specifics. Some goals are more financially focused than others, but there are always a lot of hidden details behind them.

Let's apply the Power of One to uncover the buyer's goal with the VP of Distribution and Logistics.

You have shared that the Power of One for Days in Inventory is $30 million. The next question to ask is, "What's the goal for improvement?" You likely have earned the right to ask this question since you have built credibility by knowing the company's goals; sharing how your company has helped other companies in the same industry; made observations regarding the company's financial performance; and introduced the Power of One.

Let's say the response is, "Five days." What they just shared with you is that the goal is to reduce the investment in inventory by $150 million, which is the $30 million times five (days).

With this knowledge, you can now assess the relative importance of your solutions. If your solution can provide, say, 25 percent or more of the $150 million goal, you likely have the VP's attention. If your solution can deliver $5 million, it will probably be of interest to someone who works for the VP of Distribution and Logistics, but the VP likely would not be directly involved.

> *"I have a couple of words of advice for sellers. First, make things simpler, easier, less complex, and less ambiguous. Trying to operate in a world of ambiguity is frustrating. As a buyer, I appreciate straightforwardness and clarity. Nothing fancy—just crisp, clean, and simple.*
>
> *"Second, don't make suggestions to me and expect me to do the homework. You do the homework. I have my own homework. You're just one supplier, and I've got many suppliers. I have a boss, and employees, and customers too. Don't add to my workload—make my job easier."*
>
> **—DEAN Z. MYERS,** President, DZM Consulting, and former VP, Global Supply Chain, Operations and Business Development, The Coca-Cola Company. DeanZMyersConsulting.com

HOW TO USE THE POWER OF ONE:
OPERATIONAL KPIS

Applying the Power of One to Operational KPIs allows you to get more specific for individual buyers and tailor your message, as we discussed in Chapter 3. The process is like that for Areas of Financial Performance with the same benefits: offers insights on areas with the greatest leverage, provides a financial focus when engaging with buyers, and helps uncover goals.

To demonstrate applying the Power of One for Operational KPIs, we'll build on the earlier retailer example, just as we did for the Areas of Financial Performance. In this example, you're talking to the chief marketing officer (CMO). You sell solutions that provide deeper customer insights. From Chapter 4, you know that one of the goals is to grow revenue, especially digital sales, by implementing initiatives such as enhancing omnichannel capabilities and social platform engagements. Like we said earlier, most companies do not publish Operational KPIs' values, so you will need to start with industry averages. To find the numbers for a particular industry, look to trade publications and online searches.

The CMO has shared with you that three of the Operational KPIs they are focused on are customer retention, cross-sell/upsell, and new customers. You have shared with the CMO how your solution, by providing more in-depth customer insights, has helped other retailers increase all three of these KPIs. It's too early in the sales cycle to know if your solution will benefit the CMO's company like they have other companies, and you do not know the company's customer retention, cross-sell/upsell, and new customers rates since these are not publicly available. This is a perfect opportunity to apply the

Power of One using industry averages for these KPIs and scaling the benefits to the CMO's company's revenue size.

The CMO is primarily focused on revenue. The profit from revenue is also important, but for this example we will focus only on revenue without going into the details, which are described in the appendix. Figure 5-4 shows the annual revenue benefits using the retail industry averages.

Operational KPIs Power of One for Retail Customer

Power of One*

Revenue Operational KPI	Benefits
Customer Retention	$14M
Cross-Sell/Upsell	$18M
New Customers	$20M

*Increase in annual revenue

Figure 5-4. Examples of Revenue Operational KPIs for Retail.

How will you use this information? A suggestion is that during your conversation, as you are explaining how your solution helps improve both of these metrics, you would say something like, "Using some industry averages, a 1 percent improvement in customer retention would add $14 million in annual revenue, $18 million for cross-sell/upsell, and $20 million for new customers for a company with your revenue." *Be very careful not to make this sound like a promise.* At this stage, you probably don't know what you can deliver. Use the industry-based Power of One to help align your conversation with what the CMO is focused on from a financial perspective. By doing this, you are separating yourself from the competition. Remember that most senior buyers think sellers don't understand their business. Using the Power of One, you are showing an attempt to know their business.

Next, ask the CMO how the industry-based Power of One compares to their internal analysis. Most companies conduct some form of Power of One internally. You are not trying to tell the CMO what these numbers should be but are using your industry-based figures as a conversation starter. Just like for the Areas of Financial Performance, a very common response is, "Your estimates are higher or lower but good enough for discussion purposes."

Now it's time to uncover the CMO's goals for customer retention and cross-sell/upsell, which almost never are made available in the public domain. You can ask what the goal is for additional revenue for each of the KPIs. Suppose the CMO says the goal is a 10 percent improvement for each KPI. Using the industry-based Power of One, you know the annual revenue goal for customer churn is $140 million, which is $14 million for 1 percent times ten; for cross-sell/upsell, $180 million, which is $18 million times ten; and $200 million for new customers, which is $20 million for 1 percent times ten. These are not the CMO's actual goals, but they do provide a pretty good idea of the size of benefits the CMO is looking for, which helps you know the magnitude of the financial benefits your solution needs to deliver to get the CMO's attention.

Experience shows that once you have gained executives' confidence, they will share the real numbers with you. But until you have the real numbers, the Power of One—along with a good story about how your solution improves performance— is a proven way to get to better understand the buyer's business and build confidence.

INSIGHT-LED SELLING IN ACTION

Action: Applying Operational KPIs Power of One

Purpose: Show the financial benefits from your solutions' improvement in Operational KPIs

Visit the Chapter 5 section of the appendix at the end of this book for more details on how the Power of One is calculated. Then use the FinListics Power of One Value Calculator on www.InsightLedSelling.com to complete this action. It contains cross-industry values for select Operational KPIs that you can apply to your customer as a starting point to measure the value of your solutions' financial benefits and have a better conversation with executive buyers. Use the code INSIGHTSELLER to access the site.

1. Select two to three Operational KPIs improved by your solutions. What is the Power of One?

2. Based on case studies, what percentage improvement for these Operational KPIs might a customer receive from your solutions? What would be the financial benefit for your customer?

3. How would you use the Operational KPI Power of One in account planning?

4. How would you use the Operational KPI Power of One with the customer? How would it change your conversations with buyers?

SUMMARY

Despite all the information available on public companies, your knowledge of their financials is still not complete and does not compare with that of executive buyers, especially during your initial conversations with them. However, you need to communicate the potential financial impact of your solution, and the Power of One allows you to do that without risking inaccurate assumptions. It empowers you to broach the subject of financial performance and let the buyer know that you are aware of the importance of financials on their buying decisions without judging their performance or sounding like a know-it-all. The high-level approach of the Power of One opens up the possibilities of discovering what's important to the buyer without prematurely zeroing in on what is not. It will get your executive buyer's attention and open up the conversation, positioning you for a deeper dive into the impact of your solution on their financial metrics.

POWER OF ONE BEST PRACTICES

The Power of One is a strong tool for getting an executive's attention and increasing interest in your solution. It links the potential financial impact of your proposition to your solution, helping the executive visualize financial possibilities. Because your competition rarely sells in this way, especially early in the sales cycle, this becomes a key competitive advantage for you. Follow Insight-Led Selling best practices and put the Power of One to work on your sales calls.

- Use the Power of One to start your high- level financial conversation early in the sales process.

- Help your customer envision the financial potential of your proposition without getting specific about their financials—keep the Power of One conversation high level and conceptual.

- Be conservative and realistic in your Power of One estimate, and never exaggerate or make promises.

- Don't expect the Power of One to make the sale for you or to drive an on-the-spot decision from the buyer. Instead, use it as a tool to differentiate yourself from the competition and help your buyer understand that your proposition has real, legitimate capacity in a key financial area, which could encourage them to prioritize it over other purchases.

FROM VALUE PROPOSITION TO BUSINESS CASE

"When it comes to business cases, I need to know the cost of the solution versus the cost of the competitor's solution. And I need the total cost—the embedded cost of my processes and the vendor's processes to support it, plus the ongoing costs.

"Then I need to know how that vendor plans to support the solution after they've made their money and moved on to the President's Club. When I'm meeting with the vendor's team, I want to know who's going to stick by me from a support standpoint. I flat-out ask, 'When all is said and done, who's going to be left—which one of you am I going to fire if this solution doesn't work?' That's an uncomfortable question for them to hear, but someone eventually raises their hand. I want that person's phone number because I am not spending money on a solution and calling a 1-800 number when there's a problem."

—**KEN MAY,** former CEO, Top Golf, and former COO, Krispy Kreme Doughnuts

VALUE PROPOSITION

THE VALUE PROPOSITION IS THE way that you talk about what your solution will deliver. It's a statement that includes the highlights of the investment. Think about the value proposition as the conversation side to the business case—"in person" rather than "on paper."

BUSINESS CASE

THE BUSINESS CASE IS THE culmination of all of your research, discovery, and confirmation with the customer about the solution and the value it provides. The business case includes both qualitative and quantitative elements and is the "on paper," more detailed version of the value proposition.

We were working with a data and analytics company. All they wanted to talk about was how many forecasts their technology could generate a minute and other seemingly impressive features. However, they didn't consider why their client, a retailer, would even invest in forecasting. The retailer wanted to have fewer stock outs and have a greater sell-through rate on what they did buy in order to avoid making a bunch of markdowns. They didn't care about or have any need for 10,000 forecasts. The key question was, how will this solution help improve revenue? The team missed the mark because they answered the wrong question. What happened?

The team did, in fact, have a great product, but they missed the point. They weren't attaching their solution to any kind of business outcomes at all.

Sellers have a tendency to get so enamored with their stuff that they lose sight of the goal and the bigger picture. When you buy a house, you buy a whole house. When you buy a car, you buy a whole car. You don't buy each individual nail on each individual board, or each individual bolt and piston. The value lies in the whole, but too often, sellers just talk about the pieces.

> *"Make the value proposition crystal clear. Don't make it hard for me to figure out why your solution is worth my time.*
>
> *"I love one-pagers. I'm much more impressed with a one-page business case than a 100-slide PowerPoint deck. Summarize everything I need to know on a page and show me that you know what you're talking about. Put everything else in the appendix."*
>
> **—STEVE CLANCEY,** CIO, Georgia Pacific

The benefits of consistently creating more impactful value propositions and business cases are that the process:

- Makes it easier for you to prioritize the benefits of your solution to align with the buyer's most critical expected business outcomes

- Helps you crystallize your thoughts

- Makes it clearer for the customer to understand

HOW MUCH DO BUYERS
WANT TO KNOW?

SELLERS LIKE TO SELL VALUE, but they don't always know whether that value is realized by the customer. A few years ago, we participated in a round table discussion on Value Selling, which was attended by many of the top technology companies. One of the topics was how much to include in a business case.

The consensus was, for 25 percent of their purchases, buyers wanted only a vision. At the time, there was a big push for digital transformation, so they just wanted some insight on digital transformation: how to do it, how much it cost, and the potential business outcomes. The same is true for AI: It sounds great, but so what? What am I going to do with it and how does that align with my strategy and further my goals?

For the majority of purchases—the consensus was 50 percent—companies wanted to know, from a high-level standpoint, the business fit, cash flows, and Return on Investment. They want to know how a solution aligns with their goals and strategies, the range of benefits that other companies have experienced, and a "back of the envelope" calculation on what they can expect. Think "business case lite."

For the remaining 25 percent of purchases, buyers wanted a full-blown business case. The lesson here is to consider the size and extent of the purchase when building your case.

Another lesson we learned, and this should go without saying, is to be 100 percent honest with your calculations. Buyers are naturally suspicious of financial benefits proposed by salespeople, and if you bring some outrageous claim to them, you lose all credibility. Be reasonable in your estimates and don't overstate what your solution can do.

Buyers don't want to hear about every line of code in your software; they want to know how you'll solve their problems and allow them to achieve their goals. That's where an effective value proposition comes in to connect what you're selling have to what they need.

More than likely, your company has a framework that you use for building value propositions and business cases, and that's fine. Standardized templates are useful, but we encourage you to review this chapter to see whether we can show you some elements that we've developed over decades of working with some of the world's largest companies, which we believe will make your value propositions and business cases simpler and more effective.

The goal here is to explain your solution in the context of what your customer needs to accomplish in a way that resonates positively for them—in a simple, clear way. Tie what you have to a business outcome the customer aims to achieve by describing exactly what you can do to help them and what some of the potential financial benefits to their business would be. You're providing high-level insights in a value proposition, not in-depth business analysis and financial analysis. The value proposition is a high-level, scaled-back version of the business case—essentially, it's the conversation that, done well, *leads* to the formal business case. We think about the value proposition as the "in person" action and the business case as the "on paper" deliverable.

Such value propositions are essential. Without them, you fail to speak in a language the customer understands. Value is in the eye of the customer. You might think you have the greatest product in the world, but if they don't understand how your solution fits into the context of their needs, you don't have a sale. Customers who don't see the value don't buy.

Crafting an effective value proposition requires figuring out what your customer's really focused on. You have to cut through the noise and catch their attention with a solution to their most pressing goals and problems, not some tangential possible benefit. Be proactive and direct in addressing their pain point. Customers are extremely busy and distracted. You're thinking about them much more than they ever think about you. Hand them the solution on a platter, simply and clearly. We can't stress "keep it simple" enough. When you're working on a complex opportunity, it's a challenge to craft a concise, simple value proposition that every stakeholder can understand. We'll show you a simple format that checks the boxes to help you put together an effective value proposition.

The big picture for you and the buyer is where your solution fits into the overall desired business outcome and the value you bring by solving the problem, instead of the cost of ownership. In absence of that context, they may simply view your solution as a commodity. Once they view your solution as a commodity, they'll focus on getting the cheapest price possible. It's a race to the bottom. The more concretely you communicate the value of your solution, the less likely they will be to expect deep discounts. To put it another way, if the customer's procurement department is asking you to knock $100,000 off the price and you know your solution is going to be worth $20 million to the customer, you'll be less inclined to give them that sizable discount and the stakeholders will understand why. You might give them *something* off, but you have to highlight the $20 million and get them to see that trying to save $100,000 on a solution that valuable doesn't really make sense.

ELEMENTS OF A VALUE PROPOSITION

In developing an effective value proposition, there are four areas that need addressing, as shown in Figure 6-1:

- The business problem

- How your solution addresses the problem

- The benefits of making the change now

- Qualifications/experience

To help you create a high-impact value proposition, visit www.InsightLedSelling.com and enter the code INSIGHTSELLER for a FinListics value proposition template.

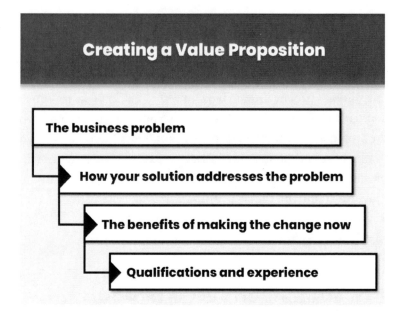

Figure 6-1. Elements to Include in Creating a Value Proposition.

It takes work to build a good narrative around each of these, but once you've done the heavy lifting, it is simple to plug your insights into this format. Let's dive into each of these four areas.

The Business Problem

This is the headline for the value proposition. You've done your homework with the customer to identify which strategies and initiatives they're building to achieve the broader company goal. Remember from Chapter 3 that a business problem is not a point solution or technology statement—it's a means to make the goal. Start with the goal and work your way down to the project so the stakeholders can understand how you're defining the problem.

How Your Solution Addresses the Problem

This is the part where you identify the solution at a high level so the stakeholders know what they're investing in. This is not a deep dive into your solution, so keep the technical details to a minimum. The most important thing to address here is the how—the means by which your solution will address the problem and achieve the goal.

The Benefits of Making the Change Now

Focus on the potential business outcomes. Keep it high level but talk about the business benefits—for example, increased customer loyalty—and financial benefits—for example, higher customer retention and cross-sell/upsell. Save the details for the business case, which we'll discuss in a few pages, but bring the potential headline benefits.

Qualifications/Experience

As a seller, in demonstrating your qualifications and experience, you would explain how you've helped others in their industry achieve positive results by improving, for example, customer retention by 20–30 percent, increasing cross-sell and upsell by 10–20 percent, or allowing them to run 10 percent more campaigns on the same budget. Keep your estimates genuinely conservative rather than based on wishful thinking. In most cases, your customer does not want to be the first to implement. Going heavy on references and qualifications establishes credibility because it shows you've "been there, done that" and have the experience to guide your customer through a successful rollout. Worth noting is one thing not to do and that's to disparage your competitors. This erodes credibility and sets an unnecessary negative tone.

INSIGHT-LED SELLING IN ACTION

Action: Create a value proposition

Purpose: Create a more customer-focused value proposition

You can use the FinListics "Create a Value Proposition" template on www.InsightLedSelling.com to complete this exercise. Use the code INSIGHTSELLER to access the site.

1. Create a value proposition using the FinListics "Create a Value Proposition" template.

2. How does this value proposition compare to those that you currently create?

3. How will this value proposition allow you interact differently with your customers?

This is where we ask you to try something new, especially as it pertains to creating your value proposition. We call the value proposition the "in person" conversation to keep your deal's momentum. You did the work to find the information to support the four pillars of the value proposition, but how do you bring it to life? *The good old role play.* Listen, we know that role plays feel awkward and uncomfortable, but they are critical to practicing and honing your value proposition. In our workshops where we role-play with sellers, it is always difficult for them at first—they feel put on the spot, they often have a hard time articulating what they put on paper, and they don't want to look bad in front of their peers and managers. After the first role play with coaching, though, they ease into delivering their value proposition with the highest executives and are excited to take it to the field. But you don't need a workshop to role-play. Ask one of your colleagues. Ask your manager. They will be happy to help. And if for some reason you can't do that, then practice in the mirror. Record yourself to hear how you sound and to evaluate how compelling and clear your value proposition sounds. Role playing builds confidence, plain and simple. Try it!

BUILD A BETTER BUSINESS CASE

Your customer builds business cases internally to prove to themselves and their leadership that a purchase makes sense for the business. You can help them decide on your solution by doing the legwork for them. They'll want to know the business outcomes, total cost, and what they'll achieve in return for their investment. They want to be fully informed. Even customers who have an approved budget want to be prepared to answer questions about their purchase.

To help you build a better business case, visit www. InsightLedSelling.com and enter the code INSIGHTSELLER for a FinListics business case template.

First, we showed you how to craft an effective value proposition; now we'll look at the components of a business case, which includes the details behind your value proposition. We're going to share with you a proven methodology that we've developed and used for many years with both buyers and sellers, comprising a five-step process to building a better business case. This process includes factors considered in both a risk analysis, such as business fit and critical success factors, and those in a quantitative analysis, such as the financial benefits to the customer and how closely those benefits align with the customer's expectations.

Business cases can be all over the map. Some companies have a standardized format or template, while others' business cases vary between lines of business and buyers within the same company. Our "tried and true" format is derived from many years of building hundreds of business cases for the seller and working with companies to build them from the buyer's side as well.

"A VP of finance or a CFO looks at a value proposition or business case differently than a VP of supply chain. A seller should understand the various lines of business, their goals, strategies, and initiatives, and tailor the message accord-

ingly. With large deals, there are going to be many stake-holders, so this is a rule rather than an exception."

—TOM SCHMITT, Chairman, President, and CEO,
Forward Air Corp.

Depending on the individual you're working with, some buyers tend to give more credence to business cases than others. For example, finance people will likely be skeptical and apt to question the numbers regardless of your due diligence. Executives from other business units may, on the other hand, be delighted with a business case that saves them time and helps them to socialize the idea. Whatever your buyer's attitude toward business cases, don't let that stop you from learning the basic methodology presented in this chapter. Even if you don't plan to prepare a formal business case, understanding the methodology will help you get a better handle on your buyer's thoughts, priorities, and expectations and will assist your conversations as you work through the details of a potential deal.

The buyer is always comparing your solution to the competition. Think about how much more powerful your proposal looks when you provide the "how and how much," which are typically unknowns with the competition because the competition doesn't frame their solution this way. Granted, the buyer has their own internal process to measure benefits, but you can guide them to the numbers that you deliver on and save them some effort. Helping them understand both the qualitative and quantitative value and the "how and how much" can accelerate the deal.

IF YOU'RE LOOKING TOO HARD,
YOU'RE ON THE WRONG PATH

A SOLUTION CONSULTANT WE WORKED with was internally engaged with a company, helping them make the right buying decision around a particular solution. At first glance, the solution looked good, but knowing the expectations of the CMO and CFO, we encouraged them to dig deeper before recommending it. Upon further inspection, the consultants realized the numbers the solution delivered weren't going to be high enough to impress those executive buyers.

Regardless, they kept working on the business case, making assumptions around the fully loaded cost versus incremental cost and asking themselves whether, if they were the buyer, they'd be willing to pay more for the solution. With some considerable massaging, they were showing excellent return and Payback. Just as the team was getting excited about the prospects of the deal, we asked them, "Hold on, folks. You know what's really bad about building business cases? You start believing your own bullshit."

Even though they weren't actually making anything up, they were looking too hard for the answers. They agreed that they needed to back up and could not move forward with the case.

If you find yourself making too many assumptions or stretching to make a connection between your solution and the buyer's expected business outcome, you're probably going down the wrong path. As our example shows, it's not only sellers that do this—even buyers themselves, and their consultants, are prone to making assumptions in order to make a solution "fit."

When in doubt, err on the side of underexpecting, underpromising, and overdelivering. Even when you consider that most buyers seldom revisit their original expectations to see if the actual value realized as what was originally promised, there is no reason to abandon due diligence. Don't embellish the facts. Don't introduce unlikely scenarios or make questionable assumptions. And whether you're building a business case for a customer or evaluating one for an internal client, never believe anyone's bullshit—including your own.

Some form of a business case is useful in any deal. The case for a $100,000 deal will not be as detailed as those for multimillion-dollar deals, but in every case, you need to show the buyer your solution's business outcomes and present a compelling reason for them to act. The question is, how much do you want to participate in this process? There is a danger in providing too much information or overengineering the business case to the point that it's not useful. Your customer knows what they need, and giving them more than that is a distraction. You need to walk the fine line between not enough and too much. They don't want to see an overly technical, overwhelming case full of spreadsheets and pivot tables. That is not going to resonate.

Make yours high level, take into account all the assumptions you've learned from previous conversations, and focus on the business outcomes the client expects. They are still going to do their own homework and prepare their own case, but you can make their work easier.

Not all buyers expect you to prepare a business case, but if you do it right, they will appreciate the work. You need to find the "headlines" to get their attention and be relevant to them.

Figure 6-2 shows the five steps to building a business case. Let's explore each step in detail.

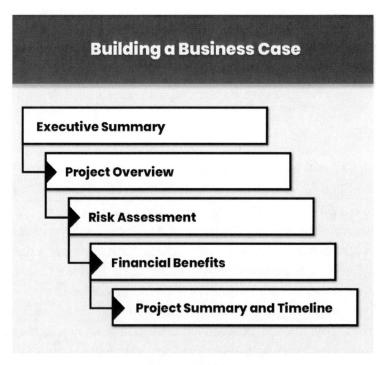

Figure 6-2. Elements to Include in Building a Business Case.

Executive Summary

The executive summary describes the specific areas for improvement. This could include the supply chain, manufacturing, marketing, or sales, for example, or a combination of these lines of business. Tie the solution, as it relates to those functions, to their initiatives that are supporting strategies and overall company goals of the project.

The executive summary also includes a summary of findings. Say you're focused on a customer's sales organization. Based on your research, you might discover that the customer's sales team's close rate is 20 percent, while the industry average is 30 percent. Your summary of findings might include that information, along with the cause for the discrepancy, your proposed solution, and finally, how improving the close rate to 30 percent will impact the sales department's metrics and goals.

The executive summary also includes a summary of the assessment of the project's risks as well as financial benefits.

Bear in mind that executives are busy. They may not read the entire business case; in fact, many of them will only read the executive summary, so you have to hit them with the facts of how your solution will impact their business early in the conversation and the presentation. They are not interested in cliffhangers, but if you tell them where you're going from the start, they will hang in there to find out how you get there. One of the executives we interviewed said ideally the executive summary is on one page. Now, that's being clear and getting to the point!

Next, the project overview describes the problem and what you are proposing in more detail. Again, clearly articulate the problem your solution addresses in terms the buyer understands before you jump into the numbers. Tie it to the company's strategies and goals. Explain how you researched the problem and came up with the solution. For example, the company might have a goal of improving overall profitability to generate cash to reinvest in the business. They believe they have an opportunity to do that by improving operational efficiencies. So your project overview focuses on the problem of operational efficiencies, and your methodology includes talking to people within the individual plants, stores, or departments to understand how they currently do their jobs. The methodology can't be limited to a small group of constituents; it should be a well-rounded, multiperspective investigation to provide a true picture of the company's current situation.

This section also includes what we like to call "How does it work?" You have to tell the buyer how your solution works. Without getting into the technology weeds, explain how the solution does what it does. Your customer, for example, has a goal of growing revenue. As a part of this, the CMO wants to have greater customer insights to deliver more personalized offerings. Some of the challenges are siloed databases and lack of digital marketing experience. They couldn't implement a solution to garner greater customer insights without first reconciling those issues. You would explain in a nontechnical way how your proposed solution will resolve the issue of siloed databases. And it also includes services to support the digital marketing and analytics, as well as the knowledge transfer to support both the technology side with the new data platform, the new marketing software, and the processes to support digital marketing.

Skip the technology and tell the story. Sellers usually do a poor job with this. They're in love with their solution and can't wait to talk about it. Your customer does not care, especially if they're not in a technical role.

We also recommend that you include in this section a discussion of *intangibles and alternatives*. Intangibles are benefits that are difficult or impossible to quantify. If a solution increases agility, for example, what does that mean? We know what agility means, but does it equate to faster time to market? Or something else? Other intangibles include goodwill and social responsibility, which impact branding. Unless there are measurable benefits, don't attach a specific value to intangibles. You might be able to show leading indicators, but with no direct connection to financial benefit, don't pretend one exists. Instead, figure out how to tell a compelling story around the soft value without assigning a cost reduction or revenue increase. Intangibles are important. Don't build your business case around them, but keep in mind that buyers do want to know what they are.

Alternatives are basically other solutions. Buying executives are thinking about alternatives even if you aren't. Doing nothing is almost always an alternative. No business is likely going to go out of business if they don't buy your solution. Be sure to always talk about the do-nothing alternative and the consequences of doing nothing and other practical solutions. Know what the competition's doing and proactively address why your solution is a better fit. This doesn't mean bash your competitors—be aware of them and know the differences between their products and your solution.

Risk Assessment

"Whenever a seller is telling me about all the benefits of their solution, I'm already thinking, 'This all sounds great. Now put it in realistic terms. What could prevent your solution from being successful?' I want to know the risks.

"For example, a solution is only as good as the implementation and the execution. I want to know what the seller has seen that has caused either one of those to be done poorly, and I want to understand the consequences.

"When they give me that information, I don't trust a seller who always puts the blame on the customer; sometimes it's the seller's fault, and I want to know what happened and what they learned from the experience."

—CANDY CONWAY, former VP,
Global Operations, AT&T

Assessing the project's risk is one of the most important parts of a business case. Yet, our experience is that it is often poorly done. There are several sources of risk. Some are internal, which we will review, and others are external such as those explored in Chapter 2, which were operational, customer, and economic risks.

The information you provide in the risk assessment earns you the right to discuss the financial benefits. For example, if your solution does not align with at least one of the customer's goals, the financial benefits are not relevant.

When we ask sellers, "When you hear the phrase 'business

case,' what's the first thing that comes to mind?," the most common responses are things such as Return on Investment, Payback, and financial justification. These are all important, and without them, a project is not likely to get funded. But the assessment of risk is also very important. We have built many business cases, and our thoughts are that the risk assessment is just as important as the financial benefits.

To help with the risk assessment, Figure 6-3 includes a list of common project critical success factors. Critical success factors are factors that must go well for a project to be a successful part of the overall risk. Identify the risks and address any potential area of failure. The short version of this is to do your homework and be prepared to answer these questions around each factor, illustrated in Figure 6-3:

1. **Strategic business fit:** Which goals and strategies does your solution support?

2. **Organizational support:** Is the project a high enough priority for enough of the key stakeholders to get behind, or is it simply a "nice to have"?

3. **Financial support:** Is the project supported enough that if the company were to not make its numbers or if another project came along, it would continue to be funded?

4. **Project scope definition:** Is the scope well defined? Have you identified sources of project creep, and if you have, how would that affect the timeline and cost?

5. **Complexity:** Is the solution easy to understand and does everyone understand their responsibility in its implementation? How difficult is the implementation, and can it be broken into stages to make it less complex?

6. **Technology:** Does the buyer's existing technology accommodate the solution easily? What changes may be required around software or infrastructure?

7. **Change management:** Is there a solid change management team in place to execute this piece? Poor change management is the number one reason implementations don't work out. Some people's jobs will change and how they're measured will change. Has that information, and how exactly people fit into the project, been clearly communicated?

8. **Project management:** Do you have a well-defined project plan with milestones as well as a plan B to address slippage? What can you do to mitigate the risk of slippage? If the project takes longer than expected, what is the expected impact on the projected financial benefits?

Know the most common pitfalls to a successful business case so you can either avoid them or better understand why your business case didn't land. Here are some we have seen over the years. These are in addition to improperly assessing the risks associated with the critical success factors we reviewed earlier.

Figure 6-3. Examples of Critical Success Factors.

Pitfall #1: Unbelievable Returns

Promising a client unbelievable, or even overstated, returns is a sure way to shoot yourself in the foot. It's easy to get overly optimistic or make aggressive assumptions, but your buyer doesn't want to hear your "best-case scenario"—in fact, they want the opposite. Help them understand the worst-case outcome so they understand the exposure. If your magnificent business case promises 4,000 percent ROI, step back and ask yourself, "Is this believable?" We don't need to tell you, "No, it's not."

If you're talking to a buyer in the finance department, they will go right to those numbers as a quick "sanity check," and if they don't check out, they won't believe another word that comes out of your mouth. Look at the return because that's what they're seeing first. And if you do have an incredibly high return, preface it with a comment letting them know that you realize how high it is: "Customer, I know a 1,000 percent ROI seems unbelievable, so let me tell you why it's this high." Keep in mind that this is the exception. Your numbers will typically be believable; if they aren't, check your key estimates of the project's financial benefits and costs.

Pitfall #2: Too Much Reliance on Intangible Benefits

Both the qualitative and quantitative benefits matter, but a case that's too reliant on soft costs or cost avoidance lacks substance. A buyer versed in finance will cringe if that's your biggest headline. As one customer noted, "Great, you're giving me happy employees. What does that do to productivity and turnover? I need the numbers."

PITFALL #3: POOR TRACKING AND ANALYSIS OF RESULTS

A satisfied customer continues to buy from you. Yet, sellers—and even buyers—often lose sight of the initial agreement. Recognize up front the importance of tracking and analyzing what you said your solution will do versus what actually plays out. We call this *value realization*. Without a process for this task, you and the customer will not likely remember what was proposed. This is a missed opportunity to identify the true value of your solution—information you can leverage long after the deal. This step is especially critical with subscription-based solutions that a client can cancel; without continuous reminding of the benefits delivered, they may not be aware of them. This trend also accounts for the explosion of Customer Success teams in recent years. Their purpose is to ensure continued customer satisfaction, including reminding the customer about the ongoing benefits of a solution or service.

When you neglect tracking and analysis, your buyer has nothing to tell the CFO who asks, "What ever happened to that million dollars I gave you? Did we get the results you expected? When and how much?" The days of glossing over outcomes are gone. If you ask for a million bucks this year and have nothing tangible to show for it, don't expect to get another million next year.

Work with the client up front to establish a methodology for doing this. Not only will this inspire confidence and give you something to crow about with that buyer, but you'll also have a solid use case for the next customer.

PITFALL #4: SOLUTION AS A COMPETITIVE ADVANTAGE

Trying to sell a solution based on "competitive advantage" is a tired trope that doesn't hold water. Every seller talks about the competitive advantage they deliver. A favorite is the claim that investing in a digital transformation—by buying the seller's solution, naturally—the buyer will be able to hire and retain more brilliant millennials. That may or may not be true, but it's not exactly a competitive advantage because everyone else is doing it too. What used to be competitive advantage is now business as usual. Like the CFO at a major pulp and paper company once told us, "In this industry, we're running faster and faster every day just to stay in place." They are, but so is everyone else.

Any solution that works really well is going to get noticed by the people using it. Then it won't be a secret for long. People leave jobs, and they take the best of what they know with them to their next employer. So that competitive advantage you promised the client may be good for what, three months? Six months? Don't include it in your business case.

PITFALL #5: ANALYSIS NOT CONDUCTED AT THE ENTERPRISE LEVEL

The danger with this pitfall is that your solution may look good for one function, but it adversely affects another. You may be shifting costs or assets. In a real-world example, a seller implemented a solution that promised to improve plant efficiency. The plan included decreasing the time inventory sat at the plant and moving it more quickly to distribution centers. This just shifted the cost to those centers, which went from bad to worse when they filled up and had to rent public warehousing. The plant's costs went down, but at the enterprise level, the total inventories didn't change—the company had to pay more to warehouse them.

Salespeople want to be upbeat and talk about all the positives, but every buyer knows that projects don't always go as planned. They will appreciate your honesty with a conversation that begins, "Let me tell you about an implementation that was wildly successful and why and another one that didn't deliver and why it fell short." Don't blame the customer here either. Take accountability for the failure: "Here's what we didn't do, and here is what we learned from that experience."

Salespeople tend to shy away from admitting their mistakes to customers, but there is power in these conversations. You are showing the client that you've done this before, so they're not a test case. You have experience. It also shows a level of credibility and humility. Your client expects a certain number of issues with any solution, and if you come off like it's going to be all kittens and rainbows, they won't believe you. There are hitches with every solution or with the implementation of the solution, and how you and your team show up in those moments of "project yellow and red" tells the customer a lot about who you are and whether they want to continue working with you. Risk as a whole category is qualitative, but being able to anticipate and feel secure within a risk profile is extremely important to the client.

COMPANY CULTURE:
THE INVISIBLE DEALBREAKER

A company's lack of capacity for change can bring an otherwise perfect business case to a screeching halt. Consider the culture you've experienced before putting together a case that requires flexibility among the leadership and employees.

The new CEO of a large photography company, whom we'll call Mr. Eakes, brought us in to help out with financial performance. During a workshop, we noticed that most of the leadership was just sitting there with their arms crossed and not engaged at all in the conversation. We asked, "All right, let's hit the brakes. What's going on here?" One man spoke up, saying, "This is nothing personal, but I got to tell you something. We were here long before Mr. Eakes and we'll still be here long after he's gone." They literally refused to make any of the changes we were recommending, or any changes at all, for that matter.

Another corporation that we worked with, a department store, hired a well-accomplished executive with a strong background in logistics to head up their supply chain group. He was brilliant, but his senior colleagues were unwilling to change. The company had been around for over a hundred years, and in their mind, there was no reason why they would not be around another hundred years. Just about every recommendation brought by this man was met with the same response, "We've already tried that. We already know that. We did that before," when it was obvious that they had not.

In the end, one company ended up with only a fraction of the revenue it had at its peak and the other company filed for bankruptcy. The lesson is that you can't help a company that doesn't want help. Save yourself some time and find a customer that is open to your business case—and doesn't want to go bankrupt.

Financial Benefits

"When building a business case, sellers should include the time commitment and Opportunity Costs for the internal staff. A lot of times that gets excluded, and leaving it out overstates the project's financial benefits. These people are very busy—their time is valuable—and should be included in the quantitative benefits of a solution."

—JUSTIN HONAMAN, former VP/GM, Analytics, Data & Digital Transformation, Strategic Sourcing & Procurement, Georgia Pacific

Once you've completed the risk assessment and convinced the customer it's a credible idea, you've now earned the right to talk about the financial benefits of your solution. Again, you have to earn that right. Never lead with the numbers. Follow the steps for a solid risk assessment first, and your customer will be open to listening to the project's financial benefits.

Your solutions deliver financial benefits by improving a customer's cash flow. Figure 6-4 gives you some ideas for how your solution might increase the buyer's cash flow.

DON'T FORGET THE USERS

EMPLOYEE READINESS AND ACCEPTANCE OF a new solution is unpredictable and sometimes surprising. Take an enterprise asset management solution that was rolled out to track the performance of the company's operating assets. Employees were provided with tablets for inputting data digitally. The financial benefits would have been phenomenal—if people used the tablets. The problem was that they were still attached to the old clipboards they'd been using for years. They were used to writing everything down manually and did not want to change. What was worse, they'd collect the data and only use a part of it to better manage the assets. A reluctance to give up pen, paper, and clipboard for a shiny new tablet isn't a challenge you're likely to consider when building a business case, but these kinds of issues with employee readiness are common.

In this example, we can't blame the seller for what was apparently a failure of change management within the company. However, the seller could have anticipated the problem if they had had a better understanding of the company's leadership and culture.

REGULATORY REQUIREMENTS:
THE ULTIMATE OPERATIONAL RISK

YOU NEVER KNOW WHEN A company might throw you a serious curveball. At a proposal meeting, a seller stepped through their plan to implement drones to inspect certain parts of the customer's factory. They had the drone company lined up and all the wireless transmission worked out. It would save the business a lot in labor costs, plus deliver more real-time information. It was perfect until they brought it to the plant manager, who informed them that their union's laws outlaw the use of drones in factories.

REVENUE

Improve customer insights with the solution, allowing them to grow their revenue. In this case, the cash flow is due to an increase in profits from the increase in revenue. Marketing and salespeople in particular are interested in the revenue component, but they will also need to justify a project by the increase in profits.

OPERATING EXPENSE

The cost of investigating fraud is the necessary stifling expense for many corporations, especially banks. Using big data and analytics can help lower those costs by more accurately iden-tifying transactions that are fraudulent, with fewer or no "false positives" that the company would otherwise spend money investigating. Chatbots replace human interactions with customers. A warehouse solution that replaces staff with robotics reduces employee expenses because the customer doesn't have to pay social security taxes, contribute to a retire-ment plan, or offer a health plan for robots. All of these exam-ples reduce operating expenses and increases cash flow.

ASSETS

An example is providing better forecasting services that allows the customer to reduce the investment in inventories and improve cash flow. Another example is moving from hardware to cloud-based storage, reducing capital expenditures on IT infrastructure to improve cash flow. Industrial IoT, for exam-ple, helps improve Capacity Utilization and extend produc-tion assets' useful life which lowers capital expenditures and increases cash flow.

Net Cash Flow refers to the sources of cash flow bene-fits such as those shown in Figure 6-4 less the project's costs. Although the financial decision-making metrics are largely driven by Net Cash Flow, you can view them along three differ-ent dimensions: return, Payback, and valuation. A simple way to look at this is to compare it to a buying decision you might make for your own home, such as installing solar panels. The return would be the savings on your utility bill compared to the cost of the investment, the Payback would be how long it takes to get your initial investment back, and valuation would be the increase in home value. Let's explore the common financial criteria used in a business case. See the appendix for more detail.

Examples of How Solutions Increase a Customer's Cash Flow	
Revenue	**Operating Expense**
Greater customer insight drives more **revenue** and **profits from revenues** increases cash flow	Big data and analytics lower **fraud expense** increasing profits and cash flow
Assets	**Assets**
Improved forecasting lowers **inventory safety stock** improving cash flow	Cloud lowers capital expenditures on **infrastructure** improving cash flow

Figure 6-4. Examples of How Solutions Increase a Customer's Cash Flow.

RETURN

How much return will you get relative to the cost? This is called Return on Investment, which is commonly referred to as ROI: "R" "O" "I." Suppose you propose a project that is expected to deliver $30 million in Net Cash Flow over the next three years. The total cost over the next three years is $10 million. This is a 300 percent ROI, which is the $30 million in Net Cash Flow expressed as a percentage of the $10 million investment. Thought of another way, for every dollar invested, you get $3 back.

That's the first step, but companies typically have many projects vying for resources, so they will want to know more than the simple ROI. They will want a return measure that takes into account the timing of the Net Cash Flow. A project that delivers more Net Cash Flow earlier on has a higher return than one that delivers most of its Net Cash Flow later on in the project. Without going into all the details, this is what is called Internal Rate of Return, or IRR: "I" "R" "R." It's like an average annual return account for the timing of the Net Cash Flow. If you want to learn more about IRR, see the appendix. It's also a great cure for insomnia!

PAYBACK

How quickly will the customer get their money back? Looking at the energy-efficient window example, Payback is how soon you recoup your $2,000 investment. Saving $100 a month on your utility bill will give you a Payback in twenty months. A company looks at this as "When do I recoup my money and start making a profit?" For example, a project costs $10 million and provides cash flow benefits of $5 million per year. At the end of the second year, the customer has recouped the $10 million investment resulting in a two-year or twenty-four-month Payback. A customer typically expects Payback in twelve months or less, and eighteen to twenty-four months for complex projects. You'll also find that during times of economic or global uncertainty, companies ask for shorter Payback times. See the appendix for more information on Payback and examples.

VALUATION

What value will the project create for the company? High-level executives will want to know the Net Cash Flow, or how much cash the project generates. They may have a minimum before they even show interest. A director may show interest at a lower number. A more sophisticated measure is Net Present Value, or NPV: "N" "P" "V." This accounts for when Net Cash Flow is delivered and the customer's cost of money. NPV is one of the most commonly used measures of a project's value. NPV considers the fact that the money received in Year 3 or Year 4 is not worth as much as the money received in Years 1 and 2, because if the company had it sooner, they could invest it to grow in value. Basically, it's the common financial adage that a dollar today is worth more than a dollar tomorrow.

With this in mind, what are ways that your solution can more quickly deliver up-front cash flow? Or how can your solution better match the project's cash flow benefits with the project's costs? One of the benefits of cloud solutions, for example, is that they better match a project's benefits with costs when compared to the traditional—and now becoming old-school—way of heavy up-front investment, say, in hardware and software. Benefits and costs being the same, cloud solutions deliver higher NPV.

How often have you proposed a solution that has all the right risk features and all the right numbers, and you client loves it, but they just won't pull the trigger? Maybe they're busy with other projects, or they have to socialize the project. When a customer isn't moving fast enough, we ask, "Do they know the Opportunity Cost of every month that they don't go forward with the project?" For most sellers dealing with this issue, the answer is usually no. One reason for the delay may be that the seller hasn't clearly communicated the value of the project.

OPPORTUNITY COST

OPPORTUNITY COST IS THE FINANCIAL benefit of moving more quickly with a project. It is often expressed as a Monthly Opportunity Cost. For example, say you and your customer agree that the net benefit is $40 million over the next three years, or thirty-six months. Simply put, this amounts to an Opportunity Cost of about $1 million a month. You can't just spring this number on the customer as a cost, though, because that sounds very negative. But you have to talk about it. Instead, frame it this way: "We could start sooner, and each month ahead of this later schedule that you're able to start, you would be gaining more than $1 million."

Make sure your customers know the Monthly Opportunity Cost. Experience shows it is a powerful way to keep buyers focused.

Delays are often caused in procurement, which likes to slow down projects to try to get a better price, say 5 percent or 10 percent off. Knowing this, talk to your buyer. Let them know that by delaying the project for those few percentage points, they are essentially, with a three-month Opportunity Cost, forgoing $3 million in benefits, which is the $1 million per month times three months. Our experience is whatever may be the reduction in the project's cost sought by procurement pales in comparison to the Opportunity Cost.

If you have not used Opportunity Costs in selling your solutions, then try it. We bet you are pleasantly surprised with the results.

PROJECT SUMMARY AND TIMELINE

Finally, the project summary and timeline explains the scope of the project. You may not be proposing a solution for all twenty-five of the client's plants or their 5,000 stores, but you are proposing, in this business case, an implementation at five plants initially, or a hundred stores. Include what that will require from the client and the expected outcome. There may be a change management piece that needs to be addressed, and the client needs to know that. Tell them what you need from them for a successful rollout, how long it will take to complete, and the milestones along the way.

SUMMARY

The value proposition and business case creation are some of the most important components of Insight-Led Selling because when you've gotten here, you've built credibility, got the stakeholders' attention, and progressed the deal to serious consideration. You may have eliminated competition along the way. And it's all pretty simple too. All it takes is some research up front, filling in the blanks and validating your assumptions with the customer, and using the value proposition format and business case template. Keep in mind, putting this into motion may feel uncomfortable at first, but once you practice and deliver a few times and see success, it will become habit.

And don't forget to visit www.InsightLedSelling.com, code INSIGHTSELLER, to download the FinListics value proposition and business case templates.

VALUE PROPOSITION TO BUSINESS CASE BEST PRACTICES

You'll have more success with executive buyers when you create value propositions and build business cases focused on the customer's desired business outcomes instead of selling on features, functions, and cost. Insight-Led Selling best practices will help you better communicate the real value of your solutions.

- Always think customer first. What are their problems, their opportunities, and their needs? Start here, *always*.

- In your value proposition, get right to the point. Have the elevator pitch mindset— meaning you should be able to powerfully explain your business and financial benefits very quickly and at a very high level.

- Don't go too deep into your technology, its features, or functionality. Remember to first demonstrate how what you are proposing delivers business outcomes.

- For a business case, remember executives view projects in terms of risks versus benefits. Help them understand the risks and give them a realistic view of the potential business and financial benefits.

- Provide examples where your solutions have provided business outcomes for other customers like those outcomes your client wants to achieve.

CONCLUSION

"Scripting from mentors or company playbooks is extremely useful in laying the foundation of a seller's financial vocabulary. However, there will be moments when you have to depart from a script and think on your feet. If that's daunting in the beginning, don't be afraid to be human and just tell your buyers up front, 'Look, I can't expect to be as fluent in corporate finance as you are, but here's what I know we can help you with.' We can tell when you're faking—we would rather you just say if you're not sure about the vocabulary. You might even build better rapport while also learning the language."

—NATHAN DANE, CFO, Intent Solutions

Our mission with this book is to help you understand your customers from the many dimensions affecting their buying decisions. We hope you start putting what you've learned to work right away. Becoming an Insight-Led Seller doesn't require weeks, months, and years of study, and you don't have to know how to speak with every buyer, at every organizational level, and within every industry and line of business. Just remember the three main themes: (1) Tell them something they don't know; (2) Deliver business outcomes, which include both operational and financial benefits; and (3) Make their life easier. This approach will deliver measurable results and guide you toward becoming an Insight-Led Selling pro. It will move you up the hierarchy from vendor to trusted advisor and eventually, strategic partner. And along the way, you will learn how to speak with many different buyers, become more informed, and gain valuable insights that you can leverage with every new customer and in each new conversation.

Of the three themes, delivering business outcomes can be the most difficult to implement, and that's why much of this book focuses on simplifying the process. Specifically, connecting the financial benefits of your solution to a customer's initiatives and, by extension, their strategies and goals can be an intimidating ask, yet a working knowledge of finance as it relates to business outcomes is critical to any sale. Our goal is to make the topic much less intimidating—and more useful— by stepping through finance in practical ways from the viewpoints of executives and others at various organizational levels and in different industries and business units. All these people are potential buyers. The more you understand finance, the better you will understand their unique strategies, goals, and other motivators behind their buying decisions.

EVERY DIMENSION, CHAPTER BY CHAPTER

In Chapter 1, "Executive Insights," you learned that to sell to executives, you have to think like one. This chapter provided insights into how executives think and ultimately what they expect from you as a seller. They want you to tell them something they don't know, deliver business outcomes, and make their life easier. They do not want to be sold to—they want to understand how you can help them achieve business outcomes they were focused on before they even heard of you.

Chapter 2, "Industry Insights," showed how the main driver of a company's performance is strongly influenced by its industry's performance. Executives expect you to understand the nuances of their industry, such as business and technology trends, and how you can help them leverage those trends. They want you to understand the industry risks and demonstrate how you can help them manage those risks. Being fluent in a company's industry-specific speak raises your credibility and sets you above the competition. The information in this chapter provided a framework to create industry-specific playbooks that help get sellers, Marketing, and others on the same page regarding your solution's business outcomes benefits and targeted buyers.

Although you should always look to improve existing relationships within your customer base, Chapter 3, "Line of Business Insights," explored the priorities that exist within other functions that you may not be accustomed to addressing. The buying landscape has changed, and selling only to people in charge of technology, for example, isn't enough. Open up the aperture and understand that other stakeholders are often involved. Learn their responsibilities for delivering on goals and how your solution can impact them. Even when different functions are aligned to a shared goal, the people involved may have different strategies and measures of success—and they may even be competing with others' measures. Knowing what's on each stakeholder's dashboard empowers you to identify the value to each function and tailor your message accordingly. In other words, when you talk to Operations, talk operations. When you speak with the CMO, speak marketing. It's not enough to say to everyone, "I can help your business grow." To these individuals, that kind of statement means nothing.

In Chapter 4, "Financial Insights," we showed you why managing financial performance is one of *the* most important—and in many cases, the most important—job for executives. Financial performance cuts across all organizational levels, industries, and lines of business. Seeing it from each buyer's perspective and communicating how your solution can improve financial performance within each individual's specific area is one of the most powerful tools you can bring to a conversation. This may seem like a daunting task, but in each industry the reality is, there are just a handful of critical metrics that drive a company's financial performance. Identify those metrics, know which ones you can influence and enhance, and learn to communicate that to your buyer. You do not have to be a financial expert. You do have to know *how* your solution can impact those metrics and have a general idea of *how much* it impacts them.

"The Power of One," the subject of Chapter 5, gave you a starting point for discussing your solution's effect on financial performance. This approach allows you to add a financial dimension to the conversation early in the sales process, which captures the buyer's attention and encourages them to be more open to speaking with you about what they want from your solution from a financial perspective. Even a small improvement can deliver a major financial impact, and the Power of One illustrates the possibilities. It is not a commitment or a promise but a way to identify areas of opportunity and the potential impact.

Chapter 6, "From Value Proposition to Business Case," put all the pieces together to give you a framework to start using Insight-Led Selling while you learn and develop your skills. Start with this framework, plug in what you know, then do your homework to fill in the blanks. Do your own research, pull in your colleagues to help, and speak with your customers. With this framework for building value propositions, there is no excuse to delay putting Insight-Led Selling into action. Developing a value proposition is essential for communicating the business and financial value of your solutions.

USE IT OR LOSE IT

Insight-Led Selling that stays in your head and isn't put into practice doesn't do you or your company any good. Take it out into the world and to your customers. Start using it right now—today, on your next sales call. It may feel uncomfortable at first, but Insight-Led Selling is like a muscle that you haven't worked in a long time, maybe never. Get out there and flex. The more you use this method, the more fluent you will become. It gets easier, and you'll see success, and you'll gain more confidence in it and in yourself. Insight-Led Selling will change your client relationships. It will change your career.

Get your colleagues involved and make it a team sport. Use your shared brain power to explore, research, and test better ways to talk to customers. Articulate the message for customers at every organizational level and in every stakeholder's line of business in your primary industry. Practice speaking about how your solution is consistent with their goals and strategies, and how it can benefit their financial performance.

Choose one client and learn and apply the different dimensions: executive and managerial level, industry, and business unit. Learn about their financial considerations, then use the Power of One to build a better business case. If you can improve one of the customer's financial metrics by 1 percent, what would that mean? What kind of impact would they see if you improved two or three metrics by a percentage point? Figure that out and commit to using what you learn in your next conversation.

BEFORE YOU GO

To help you with your journey, we have more to share. Resources are available on the *Insight-Led Selling book site at* www.InsightLedSelling.com and accessible with the access code INSIGHTSELLER. Also, visit us at www.finlistics.com for Insight-Led Selling-related blogs and white papers, and to get a demo of ClientIQ, our sales intelligence platform. You might want to check out what our customers and users are saying about us on G2 crowd at www.g2.com. And of course, you can find us on LinkedIn and Facebook. Follow us there for the latest.

If you need more personalized assistance, reach out to us at finlistics.com or by email at info@finlistics.com.

Whether you need more help, or you've mastered our techniques, let us know how Insight-Led Selling is working for you. We'd love to hear about your challenges and your successes. And we always want to know what more we can do to make Insight-Led Selling easier for sellers like you.

—Dr. Stephen Timme and Melody Astley, May 2021

INSIGHT-LED SELLING BEST PRACTICES

Congratulations on reaching the end of this book! But this isn't the end; it's the start of a whole lot of new sales wins. We'll leave you with some key points to remember, but if you need more help, please don't hesitate to reach out at info@finlistics.com.

- Instead of leading with your company, product, technology, features, or functions, always start with the customer and seek to gain insight into a specific problem they are trying to solve or goal they are trying to achieve.

- Customers have goals, strategies, and initiatives, and their success is measured by financial and Operational KPIs. Learn them by industry, by line of business, and by each stakeholder in the deal.

- Discover your customer's desired business outcome and show them how your solution can help them make it a reality.

- Show them how and how much.

- Enlist your colleagues to gather and share industry and line of business information to add to your knowledge base so you'll have a go-to manual for starting the high-level conversation with every new customer.

- Never think you can't do this. You can. If you've been in the sales business for a while, you already know much more than you think you do. Simply being aware of the insights you need to succeed will open your eyes and ears to a plethora of new knowledge that has always been there, even though it may seem like you're seeing and hearing it for the first time. Have confidence in yourself, and don't sell yourself short. You're a pro.

APPENDIX

CHAPTER 2: INDUSTRY INSIGHTS

The following is the Financial Drivers Map for banking companies.

Total Income is the summation of Net Interest Income and Non-Interest Income. Total Income Growth measures the period-over-period (e.g., year and quarter) percentage change in Total Income.

Net Interest Income growth measures the period-over-period (e.g., year and quarter) percentage change in Net Interest Income. Net Interest Income is calculated as Total Interest Income minus Total Interest Expense. Total Interest Income is the interest from earning assets such as loans (consumer, credit cards, commercial, industrial real estate, etc.) and securities (Federal Funds, US Treasury and government-backed securities, mortgage-backed securities, etc.). Interest expense is the amount paid on interest-bearing liabilities such as interest-bearing checking accounts, savings accounts, certificates of deposits, Federal Funds, and repurchase agreements.

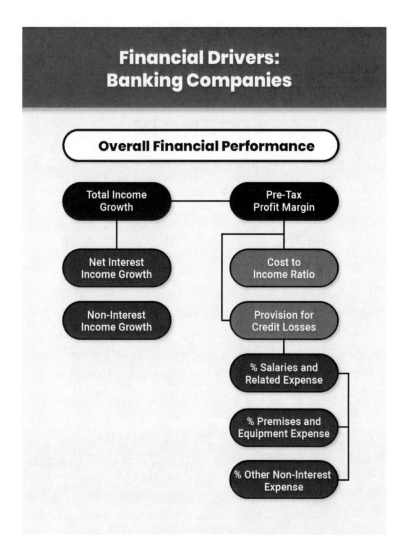

Figure A2-1. Banking Financial Drivers Map.

Non-Interest Income growth measures the period-over-period (e.g., year and quarter) percentage change Non-Interest Income. Non-Interest Income is the income from service charges, credit card fees, investment and brokerage services, mortgage and investment banking, trading account profits, clearing services, and other income-producing activities that do not generate interest income.

Pre-Tax Profit Margin is profits before income taxes expressed as a percentage of Total Income.

Provision for Credit Losses represents the losses that the bank expects to take as a result of uncollectable or troubled loans and credit losses on securities. It is calculated as follows: Provision for Loan Loss / Total Income.

Cost-to-Income Ratio, also known as the **Efficiency Ratio**, is Total Non-Interest Expenses expressed as a percentage of Total Income. Non-Interest Expenses includes items such as Salaries and Related, Premises and Equipment, and all Other Non-Interest Expenses.

Salaries and Related Expenses include salaries and wages for full- and part-time employees and benefit expenses such as medical, insurance, and retirement. % **Salaries and Related Expenses** is these expenses expressed as a percentage of Total Income.

Premises and Equipment Expense includes items such as rent, utilities, maintenance on buildings, depreciation, equipment expense on hardware, office furniture expense, and so forth. % **Premises and Equipment** is this expense expressed as a percentage of Total Income.

Other Non-Interest Expenses includes, for example, marketing and advertising, professional fees, telecommunications, brokerage, exchange and clearance fees, and other general and administrative expenses excluding personnel-related expenses. % **Other Non-Interest Expenses** is these expenses expressed as a percentage of Total Income.

The following is the Financial Drivers Map for Insurance companies.

Total Revenue is the summation of Premiums Earned and Non-Premium Revenue. **Total Revenue Growth** measures the period-over-period (e.g., year and quarter) percentage change in Total Revenue.

Growth Premiums Earned Growth measures the period-over-period (e.g., year and quarter) percentage change in Premiums Earned. Premiums Earned is defined as the portion of a premium that represents coverage already provided or the portion of premium that belongs to the insurer based on the part of the policy period that has passed.

Non-Premiums Revenue Growth measures the period-over-period (e.g., year and quarter) percentage change in Non-Premium Revenue. Non-Premium Revenue includes revenue items such as investment income, gains/losses on sale of securities, and other Operating Income.

Pre-Tax Profit Margin is profits before income taxes expressed as a percentage of Total Income.

Total Operating Expenses includes Benefits and Claims Expense; Selling, General and Administrative Expense; and all Other Operating Expenses. % **Total Operating Expenses** are these expenses expressed as a percentage of Total Revenue.

Benefits and Claims Expense includes all expenses relating to the payment of policy benefits, including adjusters' fees, investigating expenses, insurance reserves, and all other costs associated with settling claims. % **Benefits &**

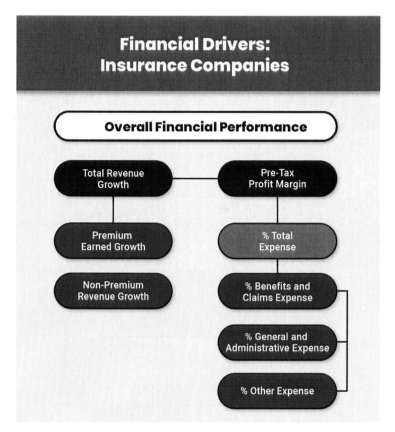

Figure A2-2. Insurance Financial Drivers Map.

Claims Expense is this expense expressed as a percentage of Total Revenue.

Selling, General and Administrative Expense includes items such as commissions, sales, marketing, information technology, human resources, and finance and accounting. **% Selling, General and Administrative** is this expense expressed as a percentage of Total Revenue.

Other Expense are those expenses not included in Benefits and Claims; and Selling, General and Administrative and often are expenses incurred in non-insurance activities such as real estate. % **Other Expense** is this expense expressed as a percentage of Total Revenue.

CHAPTER 3: LINE OF BUSINESS INSIGHTS

The figures in this section are examples of the Buyers Alignment Framework for banking and insurance companies.

CHAPTER 5: THE POWER OF ONE

The Power of One as it relates to Areas of Financial Performance for **banking** companies includes:

- Total Income Growth, Net Interest Income Growth, and Non-Interest Income Growth: 1 percent increase in the dollar amount of these sources of income.

- Cost-to-Income Ratio, Provision for Credit Losses, % Salaries and Related Expenses, Premises and Equipment Expense, and Other Non-Interest Expense: 1 percent of these expenses' dollar amount

The Power of One as it relates to Areas of Financial Performance for **insurance** companies (e.g., life, property and casualty, and health) include:

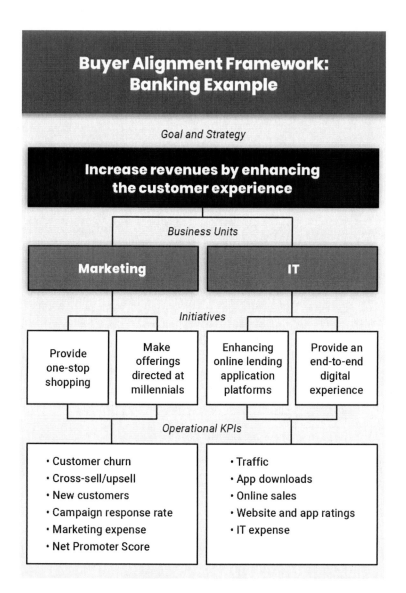

Figure A3-1. Example of banking buyers' alignment framework.

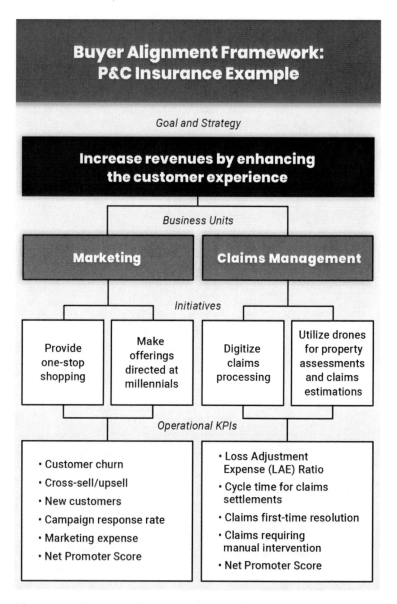

Figure A3-2. Example of insurance buyers' alignment framework.

- Total Revenue Growth, Premium Earned Growth, and Non-Premium Earned Growth: 1 percent increase in the dollar amount of these sources of revenue

% Total Operating Expenses; % Benefits and Claims Expense; % Selling, General and Administrative Expense; % Other Expense: 1 percent of these expenses' dollar amount

CALCULATION OF POWER OF ONE FOR FINANCIAL METRICS SHOWN IN FIGURE 5-3

The following shows the calculations for the financial metrics Power of One shown in Chapter 5, Figure 5-3.

- Revenue

  * **$200 million** = $20 billion in revenue times 1%

- Cost of Goods Sold

  * **$120 million** = $12 billion in Cost of Goods Sold times 1%

- Selling, General, and Administrative

  * **$60 million** = $6 billion in Selling, General and Administrative times 1%

- Days in Inventory

* **$33 million** = $12 billion in Cost of Goods Sold divided by 365 days

* In text, rounded down to $30 million to make easier to manipulate

CALCULATION OF POWER OF ONE FOR OPERATIONAL KPIS SHOWN IN FIGURE 5-4

The following shows the calculations for the financial metrics Power of One shown in Chapter 5, Figure 5-4.

• Customer Retention

* **$14 million** = $20 billion in revenue times 7% industry average customer churn times 1%

• Cross-Sell/Upsell

* **$18 million** = $20 billion in revenue times 9% industry average cross-sell/upsell times 1%

• New Customers

* **$20 million** = $20 billion in revenue times 10% industry average cross-sell/upsell times 1%

CHAPTER 6:
FROM VALUE PROPOSITION TO BUSINESS CASE

In this appendix, we explore the most common financial decision-making criteria used to assess financial benefits in a business case. The three types of criteria are:

- Return

- Valuation

- Payback

As we review these criteria, remember it is not important you know how they are calculated. What is important is that you know what they mean and how you can use them to sell the financial benefits of your solutions. Also, remember it's not just about the numbers. If your solutions do not align with the customer's goals, strategies, and initiatives, you likely won't get the chance to share how financially it's a great idea.

INITIAL ASSESSMENT OF FINANCIAL BENEFITS

Just like your customer, we first explore what we like to call an initial assessment of your proposed solution's financial benefits. The initial assessment includes criteria that provides high-level insights into if your proposed solution or project is of interest from a financial perspective.

Net Cash Flow is the foundation of all three of these criteria. Net Cash Flow is the gross cash flow from the project's benefits such as the profits from higher revenue and lower operating expenses less the cost of the project. You can think of Net Cash Flow as the project's profits. For illustrative purposes, we will use the cash flows shown in Figure A6-1, "Net Cash Flow Example."

For starters, the project cumulative Net Cash Flow must be positive. Who wants to invest in a cool idea that doesn't earn money over time? No one we know!

Also, executive involvement may depend on the amount of Net Cash Flow. Stephen worked with a large telecommunications company, and the CFO shared with him that unless a project generates at least $200 million in Net Cash Flow, he was not that involved. The point is, the amount of Net Cash

Net Cash Flow Example

	Today	Year 1	Year 2	Year 3
Project Gross Benefits		10	25	25
Project Costs	7	5	5	3
Net Cash Flow	-7	5	20	22

Figure A6-1. Example of project cash flow.

Flow provides insights at what level you pitch your solutions. Unfortunately, there is no magic formula that says if it's over this number, pitch at the highest level, and less than that number, pitch somewhere else.

Once you know the Net Cash Flow, you can estimate the **Monthly Opportunity Cost** we discussed in Chapter 6. Remember the Monthly Opportunity Cost is the additional Net Cash Flow the is forgone each month the decision to move forward with the project is delayed. The Monthly Opportunity Cost for the example shown in Figure A6-1 is approximately **$1 million**, which is the $40 million Net Cash Flow divided by the thirty-six months in the project. It is strongly recommended that you share the Monthly Opportunity Cost with stakeholders to help motivate them to move faster.

Now let's review a project from a return perspective. Your project cleared the first hurdle that it has positive Net Cash Flow. The next hurdle is, does it have an acceptable return? This is just like in your personal life. You make investment to earn a good return. It's not just about the dollar amount you earned on the investment; it's also about what you earned relative to what you invested—the return.

The simplest and one of the most commonly used measures of return is **Return on Investment** also referred to as **"R" "O" "I."** ROI is the project's Net Cash Flow expressed as a percentage of the project's costs. You can think Figure A6-1 shows the Net Cash Flow is $40 million and the cost of the investment is $20 million. The ROI is 200 percent, which is the $40 million Net Cash Flow expressed as a percentage of the $20 million investment. Thought of another way, every $1 put into the project nets $2.

Customers typically have internal guidelines for minimal ROIs for projects with different levels of risk. The higher the risk, the higher the minimum ROI. One of the challenges for sellers is that customers typically share ROI guidelines with sellers.

One of the biggest advantages of ROI is that it's easy to understand and calculate. The biggest drawback is that it does not account for the timing of cash flow. For example, in Figure A6-1 it would not matter if all the project's $40 million in Net Cash Flow came in the first year or the last year or spread out over time because the ROI would still be 200 percent. What companies often do is rank projects by ROI and then apply more sophisticated financial decision-making analysis. We will explore these criteria after reviewing another less sophisticated but very useful criterion—Payback.

Your project has cleared the positive Net Cash Flow and ROI hurdles. The next hurdle is, does the project pay for itself in a time frame acceptable to the buyer? To answer this question, **Payback** is used by a lot of companies. As we discussed in Chapter 6, it is simply how many months does it take to get back the project's costs. Figure A6-1 shows that by the end of the first year, $12 million is the cost of the project, but only $10 million has been received in gross cash flow benefits, so we know the Payback is greater than twelve months. Without going into all the details, about two months of gross cash flow benefits will be absorbed in Year 2 to cover the project's costs, so the Payback is fourteen months.

What is important is how your solution's Payback compares to the customer's maximum Payback. Sometimes customers will share that the maximum Payback is, say, twelve months but not always.

APPENDIX

Advance Assessment of Financial Benefits

Net Cash Flow, ROI, and Payback are used by many companies because they provide high-level insights into a project's financial benefits and are easy to understand. A major disadvantage is that they do not account for what we call the **Time Value of Money**. This is another way of saying a dollar today is worth more than a dollar tomorrow. Think about it. Would you rather receive $1,000 today or $1,000 next year? Today of course, since you could invest it and end up with more than $1,000 next year.

Your customer uses what we call the **Cost of Capital** to account for the Time Value of Money. The Cost of Capital is a blend of a company's cost of equity financing and debt financing. It is beyond the scope of this book to get into a lot of detail about the Cost of Capital. Plus, do you really want all the details? Probably not. For an established company, the Cost of Capital tends to range between **7** and **10 percent**. We have seen the Cost of Capital being **15 percent** and higher for smaller and startup companies.

One of the more advanced criteria is **Net Present Value**, which is commonly referred to as **"N" "P" "V."** In the Net Cash Flow example in Figure A6-1, we saw $40 million in Net Cash Flow over three years. NPV considers the fact that the money received in Year 2 or Year 3 is not worth as much as the money received in Year 1, because if the company had it sooner, they could invest it to grow in value. With this in mind, the more cash flow that's generated up front in a project, the higher the NPV. The further into the future the cash flow, the lower the NPV. Figure A6-2, "Net Present Value and Internal Rate of Return," shows the project's NPV is around **$31 million** using a **10 percent** Cost of Capital. This is in comparison to the $40 million when the Time Value of Money is not accounted for.

Internal Rate of Return, also referred to as "I" "R" "R," accounts for the timing of Net Cash Flow and is commonly used by companies. The more Net Cash Flow that is delivered earlier on in the project's life, the higher the return. Technically speaking, IRR is the average annual rate of return that makes the value of the project's gross cash flow benefits in today's dollars equal to the value of the project's cost in today's dollars. Figure A6-2 shows that the project's IRR is a little over 140 percent.

Again, don't get overwhelmed by all the details. You just need to understand what IRR is, why your customers use it, and ways you can improve it. Companies typically have guidelines for an acceptable IRR for different kinds of projects. A challenge is that they most likely will not share them with you.

Advantages of Better Aligning Benefits and Costs

Things that better align project benefits and costs help NPV, IRR, and Payback. Examples of these are cloud and project financing. These help by reducing the up-front costs and by better aligning the project's benefits with the project's costs. We can use Figure A6-1, "Net Cash Flow Example," as an example. For illustrative purposes, the project's gross benefits of $60 million and timing remain the same. The project costs stay at $20 million but are better aligned with the benefits. They are $1M, $3M, $8M, and $8M for today through Year

3, respectively: still $20 million in project cost but the NPV increases to **$32 million** versus $31 million, IRR to over **800 percent** versus 140 percent, and Payback drops to less than **six months** versus fourteen months. The key takeaway is that the better you align benefits and costs, the more desirable your proposed solution.

Net Present Value and Internal Rate of Return

		Year		
	Today	1	2	3
Project Gross Benefits		10	25	25
Project Costs	7	5	5	3
Net Cash Flow	-7	5	20	22
Present Value Factor @ 10%	1.000	0.909	0.826	0.751
Present Value	(7.0)	4.5	16.5	16.5

Net Present Value (NPV)	30.6	★
Internal Rate of Return (IRR)	143%	★

Figure A6-2. Examples of Net Present Value and Internal Rate of Return.

ACKNOWLEDGMENTS

FROM STEPHEN

To my wife, Lisa. You are the love of my life, Lisa, and you make me laugh every day. Thank you for encouraging me to write this book—and just about everything else I do in life—and for letting me still be the nutty, "absent-minded professor." I love traveling with you and sharing all those special moments.

To my son, Will, who helped me answer the question, "Why am I here?" Will, I hope you have learned as much from me as I have from you and all your buddies. Love you, Will.

To my mom and dad, Mary Ellen and Bill. So much of what I am today I owe to you. Your love has sustained me throughout my ups and downs. Dad, you taught me tenacity. Mom, you showed me that life is a journey of learning. And both of you taught me love of family and that giving to others was one of life's most gratifying callings. Love you both.

To my siblings, Ellen, Paula, Judy, John, and Lea, for all the years of love and laughter.

With heartfelt gratitude, I acknowledge the amazing college finance professors who stoked my passion to teach people the language of finance. A special thank-you to Dr. Vic Andrews and Dr. Pete Eisemann. Vic and Pete, you changed my life.

FROM MELODY

Thank you to...

Kathy Taylor, for showing me unconditional love, especially when I don't deserve it. But I guess that's what unconditional love is. So thank you.

Richard Goimarac, for instilling in me the passion for reading and writing (and Streisand) way back in 11th grade. I guess it stuck.

Jane Grant, for allowing me to observe how to methodically Maestro through plans A, B, C, and beyond. It's truly a gift.

And thank you to my tribe:

Meredith, for being my sister and my friend and for being a sounding board for all of the stories I write.

Brock, for keeping me focused and grounded. The best thing about going to Emory isn't the MBA—it's you.

Priscilla, for keeping me on my toes every day. Your creativity and never-ending drive inspire me to be better.

Elise, for unselfishly giving your time, attention, and advice with eternal patience and for having a fantastic network that helped us with the book.

Michelle, for being my COVID buddy and for being such a gifted editor. Thick and thin.

FROM STEPHEN AND MELODY

Thank you to...

The FinListics Family. You are the engine that drives our business. Your passion, innovation, diversity, and collaboration make up the secret sauce that is FinListics. We value each of you more than you know.

Becca Sundal, FinListics's very first employee. Thank you for everything you do for us all of the time; you keep the wheels on the bus, and you work magic.

Scott Hamilton and Steve Belmear, the guys who helped start it almost thirty years ago. Without your genius and creativity, FinListics would not be where it is today. We still need to take that road trip to Las Vegas.

Our clients. You are the guiding light for all that we do. It's been the honor of our careers to work with you to transform your sales teams and to deliver impactful results together. We're grateful for our continued partnerships and look forward to the many great things we will achieve together.

Our coaches, who not only help our clients' sellers speak the language of finance but also provide powerful insights from the buyer's side of the desk. Thank you, Heather Beckham, Mike Buoscio, Ben Cagle, Debbie Cross, Eric Greene, Roger Luca, Yoshi Matsui, Buck McGugan, Jacques Sciammas, and Madhav Sivaram.

Thank you to all the contributing executives for taking the time to share your stories and advice: Jim August, Steve Clancey, Candy Conway, Bill Cortner, Nathan Dane, Dawn Garibaldi, Jo Ann Herold, Justin Honaman, Ken May, Dean Z. Myers, and Tom Schmitt. It's a unique person who has the heart of a teacher—one who wants to elevate the sales profession. Each of you embody this, and we're most appreciative of your insights and talents.

Thank you, Katy Midulla, for creating all the beautiful book figures. Best of luck in your budding career.

And finally, thank you to Susan Paul and the rest of the Scribe Media team. You're a group of true professionals who made this process easy and fun. Our bucket list would be one check shorter if it weren't for you.

ABOUT THE AUTHORS

DR. STEPHEN G. TIMME

Dr. Stephen G. Timme is the president and founder of FinListics Solutions, where he is responsible for the company's strategy and vision. Before founding FinListics in 1992, Stephen was a professor of finance at Emory University and Georgia State University and an adjunct professor at the Georgia Institute of Technology, where he is still an instructor. His passion for finance led to the creation of a consulting practice that focused on helping companies improve financial performance. The practice morphed into the FinListics Solutions that we know today—a leading solution for business and financial analytics that empowers Insight-Led Selling. Giving back to the community is important to Stephen. He is on the board of directors at Camp Trach Me Away and Sunshine on a Ranney Day, organizations that help special needs children live more fulfilling lives. Stephen has a BBA and a PhD from Georgia State University and is a member of the Forbes Business Development Council. He has been published on *Forbes.com* and in various finance academic journals and has presented numerous times on benchmarking financial and operational performance at CFO conferences. When he's not working, Stephen enjoys sharing his passion for bicycling, horses, and travel with his wife, Lisa.

MELODY ASTLEY, MBA

Melody Astley is the chief revenue officer at FinListics Solutions, where she has been leading sales, marketing, and strategy since 2013. Prior to joining the company, she spent twelve years in sales and financial service roles at IBM, where she won multiple 100% Club awards and the 2010 Best of IBM Award. At Gartner, she received the President's Club Award for her work in financial services. Melody earned an MBA from Emory University and has appeared as a guest on a variety of business podcasts to talk about Insight-Led Selling and how to grow sales in challenging times. She's on the sales board of the Technology Association of Georgia and volunteers for her church's finance committee.

When Melody's not working, she enjoys cars, travel, and good wine. A self-proclaimed "foodie," she loves going out to eat and spending time with her boxer, LouLou, and Boston terrier, Charlie.

FINLISTICS

FinListics Solutions Corporation has helped transform sales for dozens of companies and thousands of sales professionals worldwide with its proprietary solution *Client IQ*. FinListics works with the sales organizations of many of the best-known technology and consulting businesses in the world.

"Buying executives want insight into how a solution helps them achieve goals and how much value the solution could deliver," explain Stephen and Melody. "It's no longer enough to recite features, functions, and superlatives from sales brochures. FinListics's Insight-Led Selling provides the business, industry, and financial insights required to speak the buyer's language."

Made in United States
North Haven, CT
12 December 2023

45332086R00169